T0209286

THE
TIMELINE
— OF —
ETERNITY

MARTIN KOSZEGI

WESTBOW
PRESS®
A DIVISION OF THOMAS NELSON
& ZONDERVAN

WestBow Press books may be ordered through booksellers or by contacting:

WestBow Press
A Division of Thomas Nelson & Zondervan
1663 Liberty Drive
Bloomington, IN 47403
www.westbowpress.com
844-714-3454

Scripture quotations are taken from the Holy Bible, King James Version. (Public Domain)

ISBN: 978-1-6642-8842-3 (sc)
ISBN: 978-1-6642-8843-0 (e)

Library of Congress Control Number: 2023900205

Print information available on the last page.

WestBow Press rev. date: 02/09/2023

ACKNOWLEDGMENTS

"I never had an original thought in my whole life," comments Dr. Michael Heiser, using this admirably self-deprecating confession as he refers to his role in making well-established but heretofore prohibitively scholarly expressions understandable for the layman (in the field of notoriously "never seen" but biblically ever-present truth about the spiritual dimension's fullness and literality). During my research for this book, and also interfacing with sectors of similarly themed primary source material that Dr. Heiser's body of work clarifies with such effectiveness, I should nevertheless offer special thanks to Dr. Heiser's mediational influence. Dr. Heiser's understatedly pivotal clarification, for example, distinguishing Deuteronomy 32:8's "sons of God" from the erroneous substitution of more modern times, "sons of Israel," leaps far above a celebration of arcane theological technicality, into the proverbial third heaven of eureka-land, opening up the real framework of the Old Testament anew. Inquire within. His work is the initial inspiration for me to use the same realm of long extant knowledge-availability to enhance my vision for the evangelical benefit that a more coherent timeline of eternity can avail. Many thanks.

Another acknowledgement is to endtimepilgrim.com author, Gavin Finley, who, intentionally without copyright, avails "for the glory of God," meticulously weighed empirical interfaces with prophetic revelation, most in evidence in this work with regard to the whole range of the Daniel's 70 weeks prophecy section, as well as the seven feasts of Israel relevance. Kingdom kudos.

Finally, kin to the above "I never had an original thought in my whole life," I offer a scattershot acknowledgment that might be called The Goo Factor. The expression, "from goo, to zoo, to you" has remained stuck in my head for years as an "author unknown" phenomenon, yet I have used it one time in this work. This phenomenon might inspire one to wonder about, of all things that remain "stuck in" our heads, what percentage of our knowledge is indeed pristinely original? Thus, I say "thank you" to every source that has had an influence upon me to produce this work.

CONTENTS

PART I

FROM THE ETERNAL PAST THROUGH ADAM'S EDENIC DISPENSATION

1

OPENERS

THE PURPOSE OF THIS MATERIAL IS TO PRESENT A BIBLICAL WORLDVIEW OF HISTORY IN THE FORM OF A WRITTEN timeline. In the interest of progressing steadily through the history, a relatively bare-bones highlighting and discussion of key events shall be used in the main text, with clarifications and expounding offered through footnotes and endnotes.

Initially, though, let us consider a question that relates thematically to this text: "How can such a form of this book's title as *The History of Eternity* be anything except immediately taken as a ridiculously presumptuous claim?" If one is aware of two truths—(1) that the Bible presents an accurate summary of eternity (one that is at least as empirically verifiable as the modern secular mythology, that ironically passes for "science" today via consensus of those who share the same fanciful feelings about the percentage of metaphysical notions that inform and steer their worldview, including ultimate cosmic origin and the origin of life[1]), and (2) it is less complicated to distinguish the Bible's superior historical framework from incorrect historical frameworks than one might at first expect[2]—then this material's title, at least in its broadest strokes, can rightly be taken seriously by intellectually honest individuals.

To touch upon a final concern before we begin with the timeline, something should be said about the fact that there are so many differing models for the story, the history, of the biblically revealed order of events (especially for beginnings and end times), so one must wonder how any model could be seen as being the most biblically accurate. For starters, the problem isn't with the Bible, but with its interpreters. The latter statement really isn't rooted in any present authorial pride; rather, it is rooted in the most often negated foundational need for everyone to accept that we must approach

---

[1] See the religion-comparing Venn Diagram with its associated discussion in endnote 1, page 109.

[2] All intellectually honest ones, including even (or especially) those who set out to study apologetics for no other reason than to disprove the apologetic conclusion, yield to the biblical mandate of repentance and proper reception of God-Jesus as Savior and as the Lord of life. Of course, those who are not intellectually honest, and thus simply have a philosophical axe to grind, cannot in that futile state of mind be helped.

biblical truth with a blank slate willingness to at least recognize that preconceptions work against the goal of allowing (fancy word) *exegesis* to do the work.[3]

This cannot be meaningfully done, for one thing, without believing that the Bible is literally true.[4] It is hardly an invitation to open oneself to doctrinal error to admonish readers to engage in earnest prayer for the Spirit's aid when examining every portion of Scripture which bears upon the subject, noting the simple and ofttimes obvious teaching of each, and observing how the various texts interpret and corroborate one another, *or not*.[5] But another precaution principle is necessary; one must mark, for example, a chosen verse's apparent degree of emphasis and clarity, as assigned to the topic of interest, and give it, as nearly as possible, the same in one's own formulation of understanding. For the sharing of even flatly *true doctrines* may sometimes be to some degree misguided in some contexts if unduly presented to the exclusion of others, to which, as one may see by their greater directness or clarity, the Spirit of God may attach even more importance. Such a long-known but less commonly practiced course, if indeed more generally adopted, would rightly reduce the great number of models that could be considered as being among the most legitimate.

The reader might also appreciate the observation, "What good does it do to present a biblical worldview, or "model," for individuals who don't recognize the validity of 'the Bible as history'?" An empirical verification of the Bible as being what it claims to be—the literal word of God—is incorporated into this timeline.[6]

*

---

[3] Simply, (fancy word) *"exegesis"* amounts to the concerted effort to identify the natural harmony of all biblical verses that are about the same topic, as opposed to the contrary effort of beginning with a presuppositional belief, and then trying to select only the scriptures that seem to support that favored view (i.e., an inferior "interpretation" ploy, known in fancy-word-lore as "eisegesis"). Lesson: exegesis good, eisegesis bad.

[4] For a discussion about why the Bible should be read no differently than, say, a newspaper, both of which use figurative expressions, and do so in contexts that make such usages obvious, see endnote 3, page 116.

[5] Since legitimate biblical interpretation is not a secular undertaking, one calling upon "the Spirit's aid" presupposes that one has already properly repented and received God's established plan of redemption, which is the prerequisite of the Spirit's aid by way of the Spirit entering the individual in the first place, and, no less, *then* also making one's way along the processional path of scriptural "mind renewal." See endnote 4, page 117.

[6] If the reader is resolved to preview one such sample of biblical superiority, see Daniel's 70 weeks prophecy beginning on page 73 of the main text, which is where its history fits along the timeline. However, the reader should also know that reading ahead in such a way would mean reading the second half of the main text before reading the first half. Alternately, though, if the reader wants to avoid such discontinuity in reading, a companion proof is in endnote 5's "Daniel's Great Image," beginning on page 119. Also, any effort along the way to recognize the *uniquely* Divine and therefore infallible inspiration of the Bible, is greatly enhanced by Josh McDowell's *Evidence that Demands a Verdict*, and J. Warner Wallace's *Forensic Faith*.

THE TIMELINE PROPER

BEFORE THE BEGINNING

In the eternal past, before any of God's creative acts, and thus before the time of Genesis 1:1, the beginningless God existed alone.[7] The first creative act of God, and perhaps seeming odd because it refers to an occurrence that is *still before the time of Genesis 1:1* when God introduced something besides himself, is a dimension of existence that includes some higher forms of physicality, meaning the creation of divine beings who are perfectly holy, the to-be-further-discussed *elohim* heavenly council, the latter italicized English translation of the Hebrew word (":אֱלֹהִים") whose meaning *includes* (among other subgroups), for example, such commonly known "higher forms" as angels.[8]

The fact of God's created elohim forms existing before the time of Genesis 1:1 is availed in the Job 38: 4a, & 7 timeframe: "[4a] Where wast thou WHEN [unquestionably occurring in the very moment of Genesis 1:1 *when*] I laid the foundations of the earth? ...[7] WHEN the morning stars sang together, and all the *sons of God* [*elohim*] shouted for joy?" (Italicized style, capitalized form for whole words, and brackets, added). In other words, these previously created elohim "son" varieties, also called Watchers,[9] are to eventually become eyewitnesses of God's Genesis 1:1 creation moment. (Readers may wish to verify such original "elohim" Hebraic usage by means of an interlinear resource, such as https://biblehub.com.)

Of course, "the most High" Elohim is the one and only Creator God, "the Elohim of elohim" as it were (as Deuteronomy 10:17 and Psalms 136:2 use, so the existence of various types of lesser elohim does not in any way at all constitute a pantheon or polytheism as promoters of the cult of The Modern Secular Mythology like to falsely claim). This speaks of Genesis 1:1: "In the beginning, God [Elohim] (brackets added)..." Yahweh himself, indeed the one and only. Conversely, the noun form

---

[7] God is/was never lonely; he was and is complete in himself. God creates because that is part of his nature; for "... from everlasting to everlasting, thou art God" (Psalms 90: 2c), "... all things are made by him [God]" (John 1:3a), etc.

[8] The main text will touch upon this topic immediately, this topic's material being corrective about the modern tendency of downplaying many (but interestingly, not all) of the Bible's blatantly supernatural elements, and this work thus being, in part, an exposé of a sort regarding the worldly movement toward a rejection of the worldview that composes the very context in which the Bible is inspired with Divine intentionality. This work indeed incorporates a degree of correction against that modern, inferior, and spiritually harmful tendency, but for a much more in-depth treatment of the whole subject, read *The Unseen Realm*, by Dr. Michael S. Heiser (Lexham Press, 2015).

[9] The Watcher usage is an English translation of the Aramaic ʻir, denoting divine or "holy ones" of God's elohim council (as used in Daniel 4:13, for example).

of "elohim" is plural, and is not a proper name, but when used in reference to the Elohim-Creator, the term, then, is always used with a singular verb.

A PURPOSEFUL ASIDE'S 1ST OF 4 ELEMENTS:

—the "1:1 *order* and *origin* status"

The above-quoted Job 38:4 & 7 shows that the lesser elohim exist at that *before*-time to the Genesis 1:1 creation, and accordingly, the yet-to-come 6-day period popularly called "creation week" must not be confused with the incident, for the six days of Genesis 1 is not *how* God accomplishes this joyously elohim-witnessed 1:1 event. The specified *order* in 1:1 plainly declares the to-be-further-confirmed absolute truth about how God creates all the starry heavens before he creates the earth, whereas during the 6 days of 1:3-31, God works on the already existing earth first, and doesn't get to the already existing elements of the heavens, including the stars, until day 4.[10] But, most telling, in addition to that latter "order" deathblow to any contrary belief, *and just as sensibly so, Genesis 1:1 is the **only** "origin" verse in Genesis 1 that declares the incident of the creation of the earth* (and, for that matter, 1:1 is also the only *origin* verse in Genesis 1 that declares the instantaneous creation/calling-into-being of all the starry universal heavens[11]).

The latter punctuation mark is rightfully known and used rather than what might be more dramatized here as a ***period***; and the validity of that latter sentence truthfully declares the supremacy of God's biblical word over all attempts to alter its plain meaning…go ahead, treat yourself, feel free to revel-read that latter sentence once again. Thus, there is no other place in Genesis 1 for the eye-witnessing angels of Job's testimony to rejoice at the sight of God calling into being the cosmic totality, which includes the present planetary element of his Genesis 1:1 project, the completely pristine and habitable earth, as is.

---

[10] So the stars are not created on day 4 (as they all are in 1:1); rather, their light is restored in full harmony with the earth again, as the unfolding timeline of the main text shall biblically corroborate. Regarding the term translated from Hebrew, "heavens," and whether it is translated as "heavens" or "heaven," the term is always in the plural (shamayim). It is exceedingly unclear why the English Bible translators alternate between singular and plural usage (for even when context is considered, there are erroneous inconsistencies); thus, one is hard-pressed to be sure even about whether such English translators knew what they were doing.

[11] That "all the starry heavens" are included in the expression, "heavens" (of 1:1, et al.), see upcoming discussion in the main text.

2ND OF 4 ASIDE-ELEMENTS:

—addressing "Day 1's swaddling-band darkness and Day 4's sealed-off darkness"

We shall continue for a moment in this jump-ahead-in-time mode concerning Genesis 1's "six days of creation" topic,[12] and we do so for the sake of presently retaining biblical coherence about the 1:1 / 1:3-31 *contrast*, thus dispelling the somewhat popular confusion upfront as a curative measure. Therein, consider *1:3's day 1* when God restores some natural light upon the already existing earth's 1:2 dark and flooded "face of the deep." We see in Job 38's revelation of such "beginning" things that at a point after the elohim presence of the pre-1:1 time, "the morning stars sang together, And all the sons of God shouted for joy." Then, at some distantly subsequent time, long after the beginning moment of the whole 1:1 history, and as shall soon be scripturally qualified, "I [God] made the clouds its garment, And thick darkness its swaddling band [in 1:2]" (Job 38:9 / brackets added), rendering the opposite sight of what 1:1 is in the beginning. This day 1's indeed *physical* restoration of planetary light (i.e., composed of particles and waves, and thus the means whereby the light of "Day" for all time going forward is so-definitively occurring in verse 5[13]) is a restorative act upon our mentioned "thick darkness…swaddling band" that engulfs the earth at the time of 1:2.

Thus, day 1 is not a complete restoration of light, for, day 4's restoration of the different type of light—specifically, *sealed-off* light from the sun and from the other stars—did not occur on day 1. (And of course, then, as shall be further established, neither was such sun and starlight sealed-off in the originally perfect, *pre*-1:2-swaddlingband world of 1:1.) Consider the biblical context of this sealed-off form of the sun's condition, from Job 9:

[4b]…who hath hardened himself against him [God], and hath
prospered? (brackets added)

[5] Which removeth the mountains, and they know not: which
overturneth them in his anger.

[6] Which shaketh the earth out of her place, and the pillars
thereof tremble.

---

[12] Although Genesis 1's 6 days shall be touched upon here (at the very beginning of this work) to make the timeline-facilitating point about the truth that God did not accomplish *1:1* through his actions in the notorious 6 days of Genesis 1, *the 6 days proper* shall also be further clarified when that part of history is chronologically met farther along in the timeline.

[13] This 1:3 light is to be distinguished from Divine light, as in the light of God's presence, etc.

[7] Which commandeth the sun, and it riseth not; and sealeth up
    the stars.

This catastrophic beyond-Earth sealing-off-of-Sun/starlight occurrence that takes place when all the other mentioned elements of the event described in verses 5-7 takes place is unique; it occurs in addition to the mentioned Job 38:9 swaddlingband effect, both of these phenomena referring to the Genesis 1:2 time of earth's darkness. For there has been no other time in history when all these things occur in relation to a single event. Noah's flood certainly involves great stormy darkness, but not such cataclysmic activity of verses 5-6. And even the event of Moses mediating God's judgment against Egypt, although involving a sealing-off-of-light incident, also does not include the uniquely extreme actions of verses 5-6.[14] This Job 9 revelation, then, is to be added to the short(er) list of exceptional revelations that characterizes how God uses such men as Job beyond the usual way of couching the contents of Scripture in terms and ideas that reflect the norms of the author's or compiler's contemporarily informed worldview. It is divine revelation of a long-past event, fitting in exegetically with the unfolding biblical timeline of history. Thus, in the above Job 9:7—"Which commandeth the sun, and it riseth not; and sealeth up the stars"—*both* perspectives (occurring long before "day 1" and long before "day 4") are present; thus, from the 1:2 *planetary* "surface" perspective on the face of the waters, indeed "the sun…riseth not" (i.e., this invisibility of natural light that no longer makes it to the planet "surface" is addressed on day 1), and from the *cosmic* perspective, long prior to 1:14-16 day 4, God's former work of judgmental response that "sealeth up the stars" *at the stars' locations* (i.e., well beyond the planet earth) is about to be concluded.

---

[14] This divine manipulation of light and darkness in Moses' day was particularly surgical, providing natural light for the Hebrews, and preventing it for the Egyptians, as God's word testifies, "And the LORD said unto Moses, Stretch out thine hand toward heaven, that there may be darkness over the land of Egypt, even darkness which may be felt. And Moses stretched forth his hand toward heaven; and there was a thick darkness in all the land of Egypt three days: They saw not one another, neither rose any from his place for three days: but all the children of Israel had light in their dwellings" (Exodus 10:21-23). This does not testify of any dearth of candles or lamps, etc., on the part of the Egyptians, but to the ultimate Scientist/Inventor, God, stepping into his own *physics* for his exceptional purposes from time to time (as he did on yet another occasion when he, from the earthly perspective, made the sun return in its path ten degrees, as recorded in Isaiah 38:8). "If" God can do 1:1, guess what—he can do Job 9:4-7, Exodus 10:21-23, etc.

2

3ʳᴰ OF 4 ASIDE-ELEMENTS:

—the "1:3 is not 1:1" realization

THE GENESIS 1:3 DAY 1 EVENT, THEN, IS THE DIVINE RESPONSE TO THE *PLANETARY* CONDITION, THE MENTIONED "thick darkness…swaddling band,"[15] which is separate from the beyond-earth *cosmic* situation of God sealing the light from the sun and other stars, a condition that God's day 4 would eventually address. One's honest but pre-scrutinized reading of day 4's "God made two great lights; the greater light to rule the day, and the lesser light to rule the night: he made the stars also" can, in one's mind, work *against* the established thought that the cosmic totality is created in 1:1, which, obviously, would have to no-choice-but-literally include "all" the stars of all the galaxies, etc.

And yes, in consideration of Genesis 1 usage with other biblical contexts, there is certainly no ironclad case for interpreting the associated and oft debated Hebrew words "bara" and "asah" as indicating categorically different "creating activity" versus "making activity." The point is that the real star of the show is exegesis, which must be used to make these distinctions about whether things are so-called <u>created</u> *ex nihilo* out-of-nothing, or <u>made</u> by means of fashioning or modifying already existing material, as in Genesis 1:16's "*he made* the stars also" (where translators add the italicized terms that would be better off deleted). Exegesis is a *boon* to those who recognize what unfolds here, as with already touched-upon items of the main text, as well as with other items foreshadowed here:

- As mentioned, Genesis 1:1's *order* is that the heavens are created *first*, and *then* the earth, whereas in the six days of 1:3-31 God works on the *already existing* earth first, and then afterward, works on the *already existing* star-filled heavens, legitimately debunking the eisegesis notion that 1:1 is a necessarily-to-be-perceived-as a Divinely misspoken *disordered summary* contradiction or a Divinely misspoken *disordered title* contradiction for things

---

[15] God could have remedied this earthly 1:2 swaddling band of thick darkness issue through modifying any of the different ways in which natural light sources, apart from the sun and other celestial bodies, can illuminate the planetary environment. The upcoming main text proposes one such example of potential remedy.

to come, both forms of such incorrectly perceived as misspoken disorder being, therefore, mythological delusions;

– Thus also, celebrating the truth that Genesis 1:1 is the only verse in Genesis 1 that declares the real-time creation of the earth, all other subsequent references to earth being about things done to the already existing earth or to the already existing Earth's greater cosmic environment from of old;

– The many scriptures that reveal the absolute *suddenness* in which the perfect cosmic totality, including the earth, is called into being in Genesis 1:1, temporally alienating it in no uncertain terms from the far-future 6-day extended *process*-work of Genesis 1:3-31, each day of which is distinctly assigned the perimeter of its occurrence as one step among many by means of the same day-beginning and same day-ending phrases: "And God said...and the evening and morning was the [specified number] day," necessitating that the verses prior to 1:3 are (obviously) prior to the six days;

– The simple clarity of the Ezekiel 28 and Isaiah 14 revelations of the "being called out" timeframe specifying when the being who becomes known as the devil *first* sins, *and occurring in* an eye-witnessing societal context of people, nations, and kingdoms, circumstances which are not in Adam's Eden or in any time thereafter (for the Genesis 3 "serpent" is obviously already fallen in Adam's Eden, thus not *becoming* evil and "called out" there, but *already* being evil);

– The Genesis 1:2 *Targum Onkelos* tohu-bahu "swaddling-band darkness/sealed off light" devastation that 1:1 eventually becomes, necessitating the 1:3-31 renovation to prepare it for the Adamic race;

– etc.

Having addressed the day 1 introduction of light upon the to-be-further-confirmed flooded/ devastated earth, let us, then, continue only a bit further here in this aside, to finalize our recognition of these Genesis 1 elements of the 6 days' work for what they are and are not. And to remind, this aside is indeed only a brief overview purposed to get the eisegeses annoyance (that the 1:3-31 six days is an explanation about how God created in 1:1) out of the way so that its otherwise lingering would not unduly interfere with one's understanding as the timeline continues from where we left off much earlier in the history of eternity back when the elohim rejoice about the nature of the authentically understood perfect and complete 1:1 creation of the totality.

4ᵀᴴ OF 4 ASIDE-ELEMENTS:

—"1:9 irrevocably *defines* 'earth' *as* 'dry land'"

Consider, then, 1:6's day 2, with God separating the planet's waters so that a margin of water below would remain where it is, on the planet's surface, but be separated by an air-space/*firmament* from waters above (i.e., a step in restoring the atmospheric cycle); and verse 1:9's day 3, with God separating some of the enveloping waters so that the submerged planetary surface would be exposed and become dry again—*the newly dry planetary surface being* _defined_ *as* "earth," just as it used to be the *also-definitively titled* dry "earth," as specifically termed in 1:1, *because it was created that way*—dry.

Thus, further along in the history, suitably detailed exegesis shall continue to be shared about the absolute and significant differences between God's actions that are in the real-time 1:1 contrast to 1:3-31 as their more pertinent historical segments emerge along the timeline. For now, then, this four-element aside, initiated to smooth-out potential confusion regarding 1:1 and 1:3-31, shall end here, as we shall continue below with the discussion-point that preceded the aside, namely, the entirely holy elohim-class heavenly council members being joyful eye-witnesses of the Genesis 1:1 like-perfect sin-free *natural* creation. Let's give a bit more consideration to what or who these joyful elohim are.

THE ELOHIM

This Hebrew word, "elohim," often translated into English Bibles as "god(s)," really refers to *any* occupants of the spirit world who are to eventually become known as remaining good or becoming bad. As inhabitants of the spiritual dimension/plane of existence, they are all multidimensional, thus able to also pass into the dimension of what later-created human type beings would consider to be their natural world in which the human types are temporarily confined. This is a necessity, given the fact that these lesser-than-Yahweh multitudes of elohim are created to share, in some degree, Yahweh God's authority over the natural realm ("humanoid") beings that he would create later. A specific example of scriptural documentation about a member of the "prehistoric" (i.e., pre-Genesis 1:1) elohim council aristocracy's function to carry out the above alluded-to role as servants of God's bidding, but taking place during this later spiritually fallen epoch—our The Adamic Age epoch—is in I Kings 22:19-23:

> [19] And he said, Hear thou therefore the word of the Lord: I saw the Lord sitting on his throne, and all the host of heaven standing by him on his right hand and on his left.

[20] And the LORD said, Who shall persuade Ahab, that he may go up and fall at Ramothgilead? And one said on this manner, and another said on that manner.

[21] And there came forth a spirit, and stood before the LORD, and said, I will persuade him.

[22] And the LORD said unto him, Wherewith? And he said, I will go forth, and I will be a lying spirit in the mouth of all his prophets. And he said, Thou shalt persuade him, and prevail also: go forth, and do so.

[23] Now therefore, behold, the LORD hath put a lying spirit in the mouth of all these thy prophets, and the LORD hath spoken evil concerning thee.[16]

To offer a further degree of foreshadowing, due to the *eventual* fall of some of these alluded-to pre-1:1 heavenly council elohim-class sons of God, as mentioned, the condition of good and evil supernatural forces emerge,[17] to include:

- the more powerful higher-than-angel order of *nachash*[18] (pronounced: nuh-kosh), associated with the "satan"[19] and "seraphim"[20] orders;

- the *mal'akim* (angels, and pronounced: mah-la-keem), and

---

[16] Regarding God sanctioning the use of a lying spirit, consider such a principle of usage being consistent with God's loving provision of timespans given (for those who are in rebellion) to repent; whereas, if they simply refuse to repent, God rightly gives them over to a reprobate mind that the rebellious apparently prefer (as in Romans 1:28, II Thessalonians 1: 6-8, etc.).

[17] The timing of this "good and evil" condition of opposing spiritual allegiances occurring will become apparent in the main text as the timeline progresses.

[18] In the ancient Semitic world, the *nachash* are divine beings with higher-level responsibilities or jurisdictions than angels; therefore, in the Hebrew Bible, the *beney elohim* "sons of God" are never called angels; that is, there are no passages in which the Hebrew, *beney elohim* (and similar phrases), occur as being the *mal'akim* ("angels"). The nachash are also referred to in other ancient texts, but, for example, referred to as the equivalent *apkallus* (or "Watchers," as in Daniel 4:13-17, and in a transliterated form, so-indicated in Genesis 3:1; 6:1-4; and 16:7).

[19] As true for "Lucifer," "Satan" also is not a proper name; the "satan" usage denotes one class within the many classes of elohim, and thus does not point to a specific character. Consider, for example, the common translation error of the Hebrew usage, "satan," as used in Job 1-2 and Zechariah 3, being rendered, "Satan," erroneously upper-case suggestive of an individual's proper name. The term would be better translated as "the adversary," and is not to be taken as meaning the same one every time. For an in-depth study of such related subject matter, read Dr. Michael Heiser's *Demons*, Lexham Press, 2020.

[20] This "seraphim" association shall be addressed farther along in the main text of the timeline.

-   the *shedim* (demons, and pronounced: sheh-deem, as referred-to in Deuteronomy 32:17. The translated term "demons" does not trace back to any major cultures of the Near East or Hebrew Bible, becoming established only long after the biblical canon is complete. The origin of such "demons" shall be addressed farther along in the timeline.)

As the above categories indicate, the broadest exegetic understanding of the elohim can thus also appropriately describe, for example, false gods.[21] And as a matter of fact, even deceased humans, thus disembodied and revealing our primary spirit-based nature, are also "elohim" (as used in I Samuel 28:13 for a deceased human). Additionally, Psalm 8:6 says, "You made humanity [merely] *a little* lower than the heavenly beings [elohim]" (brackets and italic style added), informing us that human seedling elohim flesh-bound beings in our *presently* non-glorified (thus non-multidimensional, etc.) form do not necessarily have to be disembodied to simply acknowledge the fundamentally high nature that shall, in the fulness of time, become much more apparent.[22]

As suggested earlier, the reader may want to use a companion interlinear resource (again, such as biblehub.com) while reading along, to directly correlate the original Hebrew usage, such as for Psalm 82: 1, 6-8, which, although also in a future context, refers to such elohim who, by the time of the discussed circumstances, indeed lose their original purity: "[1a] God [Elohim] standeth in the congregation of the mighty; [1b] he judgeth among the gods [elohim]....[6a] I have said, Ye *are* gods [elohim]; [6b] and all of you *are* children of the most High. [7] But ye shall die like men

---

[21] Some examples of false/pagan gods that emerge in The Adamic Age, and thus are **not** simply alternate God-names that refer to the one and only Creator God of the Bible, include Allah, Baal, Molech, etc.; I Kings 11:33, for example, uses "elohim" to also describe the pagan gods Ashtoreth, Chemosh, and Milcom. The origin of pagan gods shall unfold during the main text's progress.

[22] Although humans are seeded with the elohim nature, they are indeed lesser now, "a little lower" (in present abilities) than the pre-1:1-extant lower-than-God elohim. However, as specified in Genesis 2:7, this never-before-existing elohim-spirit-based nature of Adam was suddenly created by God—therefore, not from preexisting material— accomplished in the moment when he "breathed into his nostrils the breath of life," which is the centerpiece subject (yet sharing the context that also includes God's formation of the physical man, Adam, in use of preexisting material). This is a supernatural and sudden creation event. This realization invites comparison with Genesis 1:1 when God also called into being never-before-existing physical matter (for "Through faith we understand that the worlds were framed by the word of God, so that things which are seen were not made of things which do appear" / Hebrews 11:3) to compose the cosmic totality, indeed also accomplished, not strictly via ex nihilo, but via *a real something*: "by the breath of his mouth" (Psalm 33:6). This, too, is a supernatural and sudden creation event. The undeniable, but non-admitted, supernaturally founded worldview of atheism is expressed in their "from absolute 'universal' nonexistence to the totality of existence" feelings-based metaphysical philosophy. Their extraordinary claim of an atheistic worldview requires extraordinary evidence, which is still absent, although the evidence for Intelligent Design based upon the most empirically lockstep and demonstrable science that exists—the science of mathematical probability—is abundant throughout creation; this is demonstrated in endnote 2, page 113.

[Hebrew, $k \partial \bar{a} d \bar{a} m$[23]] and fall like one of the princes. [8] Arise, O God [Elohim], judge the earth: for thou shalt inherit all nations"[24] (brackets added). The various Bible translations that change (such scriptures as) the above "[1b]" and "[6a]" into references to Adamites, that is, to human beings (into Israelite rulers and judges) are wrong, misguided as the *translators* are (to be distinguished from the original *manuscripts*[25]) by the presumptuous motive to unnecessarily protect the in-all-cases unassailable and everlasting word of God from being falsely perceived as the reference: "elohim/god(s)," equating to polytheism. Note to self: Don't misrepresent God's word, no matter what the motive may be; that can't end well.

The details shared thus far suggest the question, "When, exactly, did any of the elohim indicated in the abovementioned Job 38 (verses 4a & 7), Psalm 82, etc., first lose the 'perfect in thy ways' original quality of universally unassailed righteousness that exists prior to Genesis 1:1?"[26] Since there is no scriptural basis for believing that the fall of any elohim occurred before Genesis 1:1, let us continue in the timeline's progress.

---

[23] This is the Hebrew term for "man" or "mankind," referring to the whole fallen race that emerges from *Adam*, indicative of the "$\bar{a} d \bar{a} m$" part of the above-bracketed Hebrew: "$k \partial \bar{a} d \bar{a} m$."

[24] Obviously, if the ones referred-to were indeed human being men, it would make little sense to draw such a distinctively exceptional contrast, to convey that they would **nevertheless** die like men.

[25] The method of choice by all intellectually honest scholars, using the example of whether to prefer the Septuagint over the Masoretic, or vice versa (as related to the above-mentioned "*translators*" concern), is also discussed in endnote 6, page 122.

[26] The quotation, "perfect in thy ways," is expounded upon in the upcoming main text.

3

"LET US" REFERS TO GOD AND HIS LESSER ELOHIM

GENESIS 1:1 SAYS, "IN THE BEGINNING, GOD CREATED THE HEAVENS AND THE EARTH." IN CONSIDERATION OF the pre-1:1 existence of the elohim, and of their role in administering under the authority of God, it seems reasonable to recognize here the plurality that also exists in Genesis 1:26's "Let us make man in our image" as a reference not to God's triune nature (that is indeed a valid doctrine[27]), but to God and his elohim heavenly council, in the sense of God's announcement to create yet another class of elohim-based life forms.[28] As we have seen in the earlier-mentioned I Kings 22 citation, God addresses his elohim to accomplish his own purposes at times, and in the volume of scriptures, we know that God also acts on his own to execute his own will whether the scriptures, in such additional events, happen to record any of his invocations about the presence of elohim witnesses or not. Thus, as God announces his plans (about the creation of man) to elohim in Genesis 1:26, the same "Let us" declaration from the one in charge to his onlooking subordinate staff wouldn't be an out-of-place detail (along with potentially limitless other details) at the onset of the Genesis 1:1 event—that is, *if* simple priority to get to the Adamic epoch details was not the weightier goal.[29]

---

[27] Regarding the doctrinal legitimacy of the Trinity, see endnote 7, page 122.

[28] The authors and compilers of the Old Testament, though inspired, nevertheless wrote primarily according to their own established worldview context—more naturally including the very well-established reality of the elohim sons of God's heavenly council—but which *did not include* any clarification of the far-future New Testament revelation of God's triune nature.

[29] The reason God's biblical word does not present all the beginning history details in Genesis 1 is indeed because priority is assigned to the nearly immediate introduction of the situation for readers as it pertains to the coming-soon written context of Adamic humanity, relegating the fuller and equally legitimate story of pre-1:1 elements, as well as 1:1-2 elements, to exegetic inquiry, which couldn't happen back then anyway, being without the whole canon. And, as we shall *continue* to see, such exegetic material on the topic IS included in the Bible now, as we shall continue to explore.

GOD CREATED 1:1 INSTANTLY, NOT IN SIX DAYS

The way in which, the *means* by which, God accomplishes this 1:1 creation event—and which is the antithesis of 1:3-31—is provided in Psalms 33: 6, 9a & 9b: "[6] By the word of the Lord were the heavens made; and all the host of them by the breath of his mouth … [9a] For he spake, and it was; [9b] he commanded, and it stood fast." The latter scripture's "it" (that "was" and that also "stood fast") is the cosmic totality—referring to "all the host" of the heavens, *everything* that is included in the starry universe.[30] The truth that the heavens *and the earth* are thus created at the same "he spake, and it was" time, as initially necessitated by the language of Genesis 1:1 itself, lets us realize the obvious fact that the latter Psalms citation of the creation of the "heavens," the whole cosmos, naturally also includes the Earth. The truth of this instantly created totality's status of verse [9a] that simply "was" in place at the moment of the Creator's expressed word is then reemphasized, divinely double-downed-upon in the final [9b] part of the line, thus as a make-no-mistake-about-it emphasis of having truly come about in this manner, reverberating the same commanded "it was" status that "stood fast" from the moment in time when "he spake."

Processes or unformed particulate materials (that would only *eventually* be used to form or modify completed structures of the cosmos) did not stand fast; rather, all of the specified instantaneously completed structures themselves stood fast. This scriptural revelation of the sudden coming-into-being of the cosmic totality that indeed appears from the moment of command is *even further specified* (at first seeming unnecessary, but, in light of the apparent need to make it "ridiculously obvious," as an assist to those who might otherwise be inclined to doctrinally stray on this point) as one also accepts Psalms 148:3-5, where Scripture indeed yet again informs with the same biblically inescapable truth: "Praise him, sun and moon; praise him, all ye stars of light. Praise him ye heavens of heavens, and ye waters that be above the heavens. Let them praise the name of the Lord: for he commanded, and they were created [appearing at once, of course, reflecting the absolute suddenness of Psalms 33:6, 9a-9b's 'he spake, and it was' event, and thus so obviously doing the opposite of contradicting it, as the 1:3-31 *process*-efforts *would* contradict it, except, of course, and joyously so, that the Bible does *not* teach that 1:3-31 is how God accomplishes 1:1]" (bracket added).[31]

---

[30] "The totality" is a phrase that refers to everything, and so can refer to the universe or to a so-called multiverse, although the multiverse is a secular concoction to assist, for example, in the dilemma of The Darwinian Mythology and of all its so-principled offshoots, including the concept of cosmic evolution. For further elaboration, see endnote 8 on page 123. Previously, a related discussion (about the mathematical impossibility of a politically correct creation myth, The Darwinian Mythology) exists in endnote 2, on page 113.

[31] The waters above the heavens refers to the densely composed water vapor layer of the earth's immediate "heavenly (sky)" vicinity that is referred-to in Genesis 1:6-7. The "all the stars" heavenly realm and the "heavenly (sky)" vicinity, etc., are parts of the verse's all-encompassing "heavens of heavens."

Again, mere processes beginning to act upon separated, or even upon *disorganized conglomerations of,* particles and atoms of the universe are not the phenomena created in 1:1 (and then to reconfirm, as we pointed out earlier, neither is 1:1 a mere aberrantly disordered summary or an aberrantly disordered title of 1:3-31 things to come). The listed completed elements of the Scriptures are thus created—the specified plurality of the heavens, the sun, the moon, and retain this: *all* the gazillions of stars of light themselves are specified, and necessarily therefore all the galaxies, etc. This irrevocably supports the 1:1 realization that the Earth's creation is to be included in said elements, as the upcoming new kid Isaiah 45:18 and other scriptures to be discussed also necessitate. In this creative moment, God's will and omnipotent power result in the cosmic totality product being manifest as an instantaneous expansion from God's mind's conception to its optimal extent of dispersion for the accommodation of life. Pardon these elements for the immediately subsequent mini-interview scripture, but Isaiah 48:3 says:

—"I [God] have declared the former things from the beginning; (brackets added)
—and they went forth out of my mouth,
—and I showed them;
—I did them suddenly,
—and they came to pass" (hyphens also added).

MINI-INTERVIEW WITH GOD

"Thank you for joining us."

Q: "So, from what point—*when*—did you declare the former things?"

A: "Uh, that would be '—from the beginning.'"

Q: "Ah. Well, then, am I to understand that you 'spake, and it was'?"

A: "Ah-*yourself* ! You've done your homework. So yes, '—they went forth out of my mouth.'"

Q: "Thanks for the compliment, I felt that such 'homework' was the least I should do in anticipation of our meeting. But why should *unbelievers* believe?"

A: "Because '—I showed them.'"

Q: "Let me get this straight; in 'the beginning' you spoke, and that caused what you spoke to appear…meaning that what you 'showed them' should cause tentative unbelievers to believe *exactly what*…that everything you spoke came to be, like, in a process or Darwinesque way?"

A: "That's a big negative. '—I did them,' meaning I spake and it was things, *suddenly.*"

Q: "Are you going to tell me that, well, regarding all this 'everything stuff,' you just spoke…"

A: "—…and they came to pass."

Why did God create the planetary product? As the alluded-to Isaiah 45:18 says, "…to be inhabited." How did he create it? Instantly—in Genesis 1:1 he spoke, and it was. The only other "option" is eisegesis. This is not narrowmindedness or presupposition, it's perspicuity and Bible. Those who would doubt any such biblical necessity have not harmonized all the scriptures properly, nor (or so it would seem) have they meaningfully internalized even any introductory concept of appreciating God's as-literal-as-it-gets *omnipotence.*

WE NOW KNOW THAT GENESIS 1:1 IS TRUE

Also, this makes more rational sense than the atheists' mentioned pagan religious (i.e., belief-based) notion that *absolute universal nonexistence* (which, according to their proposition, is the necessary "state of being before" nature existed) spontaneously *became all present existence.*[32] No existing matter of any sort to "incrementally assemble itself," no quantum state to mythologically "fluctuate" into a Big Whatever, etc. And, while we're at it, it should also be understood that biblical models of confessing Christians influenced by such scholars who fail to acknowledge the real-time original creation of the 1:1 totality as occurring instantly, and done so in a finality of perfection, despite such influence of rhetorical shenanigans that are afoot, are fundamentally erroneous about this topic along with such unfortunate scholars. This is an exaltation of biblical truth, not a carnal hunkering down on one side of a spurious "doctrines of man" contest.

---

[32] The author of this material realizes that many of The Modern Secular Mythology indoctrinates have "moved on from" classic Big Bang cosmogeny, but it is the model that is referred to in this text to symbolize the equally ludicrous rhetoric that underlies all models that futilely attempt to account for the totality's existence through anything less than the God of the Bible.

The elohim participation in the 1:1 event is the resultant joy, as shared in Job 38:7. So timeline-wise up to this point, God's holy and transcendent-natured elohim and a perfect, completely sin-free cosmos, including a perfect and complete earth—literally, an *entire planetary* Eden without seas—are legitimately established.[33] Why does Genesis 1:1 read like it does? Because that's when it happened. Again, there is no other legitimately understood statement or indication of the earth's creation anywhere else in Genesis 1.

"ORDER IN THE VERSE!"

If this topic was subject to courtroom procedures, one might object, alluding to a former point's development (about the order of creation in 1:1 being contrary to the order in 1:3-31), in asking, "How could all the starry heavens be created before the time when the earth was created if the cosmic *totality*—which includes the earth—was called into being instantly, both at the same moment in time?" Consider some expounding upon the earlier mentioned "instantaneous expansion" event (of page 15). At that 1:1 event, God instantaneously created the totality at a maturity level whereby, for an example in principle, our galaxy is already safely expanded beyond the distance that had dangerous radiation levels associated with proximity of materials composing other emerging phenomena. This principle of the extreme acceleration of time could, for example, account for: (1) a Big biblical Bang occurring some thirteen-plus billion years ago (in a "normal time passing" form of calculation), and (2) the Earth's subsequent "naturalistic" appearing and readying for habitation some four-plus billion years ago, but both of these elements of the 1:1 event achieved by means of being drawn out to such a universal maturity *instantly*, just as the revelatory Scriptures—which are God's words, thus from Abba Science Himself—that have been shared testify.

So, for instance, if the scientific measurements agree that some form of a so-called Big Bang (or some other occurrence) takes place long before the Earth exists, that wouldn't be a problem for the most notorious revelation of that truth: "In the beginning, God created the heavens and [then] the earth" in the time-accelerated "he spake, and it was" moment (bracket added). Of course, then, the related scriptural event from Job 38:4, for example, that uses the phrase, "I [God] laid the foundations of the earth" (brackets added), is a part of this acceleration-of-time event, as are all other associated elements of universal existence (including, for another example, the light shafts from the most distant galaxies being in place so that earthlings would be able to see them right from the start; et al., ad infinitum).

---

[33] Fear not, the above "without seas" detail of this sentence shall be accounted for in the body of the main text, farther along.

This study has already incorporated some necessary foreshadowing, "necessary" because, as we have seen, sometimes the Bible's provision of information about former things, even about so-called primordial things, is given within contexts that discuss circumstances in the distant future. So also it is with the story about how the *non*-sectioned *entire planetary* pre-Adam 1:1 earthly *Eden* came to its end, to eventually, after 1:2, be renovated into a form that is a much smaller *section* of the planet for Adam's and Eve's probationary opportunity to experience an Edenic life.

4

"THOU...THY...THEE" = T³ TRUTH

From here, then, we will return to the topic of what the Bible teaches about how the whole planetary 1:1 Eden-world became lost. Previously, the broadly applicable "perfect in thy ways" phrase is used to describe the nature of all elohim in the pre-1:1 time, and also describes this unchanged elohim state of being at least during the earlier range of time within the Genesis 1:1 epoch. The fuller and troublesome specter of this "perfect in thy ways" era of the Genesis 1:1 world is given in Ezekiel 28:

> [13] Thou hast been in Eden the garden of God...work-
> manship of thy tabrets and of thy pipes was prepared
> in thee in the day that thou wast created.
>
> [14] Thou art the anointed cherub that covereth; and I have
> set thee so; thou wast upon the holy mountain of God...
>
> [15] Thou wast perfect in thy ways from the day that thou
> wast created, till iniquity was found in thee.

Before we expound upon this and the other associated "original fall verses" of Ezekiel 28, obviously, it is pertinent to identify exactly who verse 15's "Thou...thy...thee" terms refer to; we shall start with a look at the initial target of the prophecy, the king of Tyrus. The people of Adam's whole fallen race, and thus including the king of Tyrus, are not created beings,[34] and neither are they born perfect as the contrasting 28:15 subject person is *nature*-identifyingly declared to be. *Adam's* progenies inherit the sin nature from their human seminal head himself. This truth should be enough for readers to spark recognition of the double-reference quality of the prophecy, but thankfully, such further

---

[34] Members of Adam's race "are not created" in the sense that the members were *born*, "products" of, for one thing, *biologic* procreation; Adam himself, uniquely, being created as the seminal head. Elohim are neither procreated nor fashioned from the earth as Adam is. A realization of these truths helps one to recognize the non-human/elohim-nature of verse 14's "anointed cherub that covereth" who succumbs to iniquity.

scriptural kindling for that recognition is gloriously redundant, making it unquestionably easy to see, that is, if secondary assumptions intended to influence otherwise are not one's "higher" goal. Enter the next verse of Ezekiel 28:

> [16] By the multitude of thy merchandise they have filled the
>   midst of thee with violence, and thou hast sinned:
>   therefore I will cast thee as profane out of the
>   mountain of God: and I will destroy thee, O covering
>   cherub [Hebrew: *k ə r u b* [35]] from the midst of the
>   stones of fire.   (brackets added)

The king of Tyrus was not kicked out of "the mountain of God,"[36] was not in the Ezekiel 28:13 Eden with tabret/pipe "plastic" surgical enhancements, and neither do the referred-to lines of prophecy jump back and forth after the prophetic shift occurs (thus, mythically, *from* the primordial "thou hast sinned" time of verse 16 above, *back to* the pre-shift future Adamic time of Tyrus): one moment, or so the "thinking" goes, prophetically revealing the time and circumstances of The Pre-Adamic Epoch when the "Thou…thy…thee" persona lived in his 28:15 created planetary-wide perfection of Eden, and then when a subsequent verse's detail seems too bizarre, just soothingly jump ahead in time to eisegesisly import something far less tilting, something from the much more familiar Adamic era, as in, from the sin-natured-from-birth time of the king of Tyrus era, and then back to the continuum of verses where you left off, again picking up the story of The Pre-Adamic Epoch, etc. Very shortly, we will see that this latter nonsense is a *must* strategy for anyone who is bent on denying The Pre-Adamic Age that the Bible quite plainly necessitates, exegetically speaking.

So it is true that the king of Tyrus was not kicked out of heaven; however, the formerly perfect heavenly council member—a member of the elohim, the repeatedly so-labeled and telltale "anointed cherub" of 28:14 above, this very same "covering cherub" of 28:16—is indeed kicked out of heaven after *he* falls into sin, verily, when "…iniquity was found in thee" (i.e., in him). Also, as all humans are prone to do to one degree or another, the king of Tyrus also habitually sinned in various ways, but Ezekiel is calling "the king" out for what might be categorized as a broader-based serious sin connected to the influence of his exalted, highly responsible role, qualifying him for crossed stardom—the role as host for this very flashback allusion.

---

[35] According to Strong's Concordance, this "cherub" usage indicates "probably an order of angelic beings"; yes, in the sense that it indicates an elohim persona.

[36] "The mountain of God" refers to God's literal temple of his presence; see also endnote 9, page 123.

Exegetically, then, the distinctiveness of verse 16's startling "thou hast sinned" last straw summation, and contextually directed to the subject's elohim "cherub" being—and thereby revealing the ancient *origin* of the Adamic king's *class* of sin (thereby sensibly inspiring the great human persona "shadow and type" from which such a revelation about that primordial origin of the fallen elohim being thus springs)—is more appropriately read as including the very inception of sin itself entering into the midst of the formerly perfect universal totality surroundings as seen in the 1:1 Eden-world. This, then, is the ultimate climacteric-of-evil official moment of reckoning, and indeed, one that is attributed only to the persona who is known in New Testament demonology as not "a" but *the* satan himself. The very next verse also offers some interesting highlights to this Ezekiel 28 situation:

> [17] Thine heart was lifted up because of thy beauty, thou
> hast corrupted thy wisdom by reason of thy brightness:
> I will cast thee to the ground, I will lay thee before kings,
> that they may behold thee.

Remember the previously mentioned "must strategy" about those who eisegesisly feel they must import "less tilting" beliefs into the midst of prophetic shift material? This latter verse 17 is one example of where such attempts to historically castrate laid-right-out-there-truth occurs. In verse 17, the Pre-Adamic contemporary setting of this transcendently described being's fall is depicted as a very public shaming occurrence in the midst of a societal environment that is developed to the point of the existence of kingdoms. This verse is still providing further understanding about the time and circumstances of The Pre-Adamic Epoch; again, there is no legitimate justification for hopscotching to-and-fro' the Pre-Adamic and Adamic realms to strain against the straightforward list of circumstances that are provided. With the final two verses that we will cite from Ezekiel 28, again, we have another truly redundant depiction, this time of the astonished humanoid eyewitnesses of this watershed event, the juggernaut fall of one who arguably is "the greatest" being that ever existed outside of God:

> [18] Thou hast defiled thy sanctuaries by the multitude of
> thine iniquities, by the iniquity of thy traffick; therefore
> will I bring forth a fire from the midst of thee, it shall
> devour thee, and I will bring thee to ashes upon the
> earth in the sight of all them that behold thee.

> [19] All they that know thee among the people shall be
> astonished at thee: thou shalt be a terror, and never shalt
> thou be any more.

A series of verses that reverberate these above-discussed Ezekiel 28 elements involving an earthly flashback-persona king (this next time, though, of Babylon) that also transitions, lifting the prophecy once again to unquestionably reveal a higher truth about the infinite tragedy and time of the most exalted elohim's fall, begins with Isaiah 14:

> [12] How art thou fallen from heaven [Did the king of
> Babylon of Isaiah 14: 4-6 fall from heaven? It would be
> ludicrous to conclude such.], O Lucifer,[37] son of the morning!
> *how* art thou cut down to the ground, which didst weaken
> the nations! (brackets added)

By the time of this verse 12, we have forked off from the Adamic era king of Babylon, the prophetic curtain being pulled back yet again to reveal the fall of the premier elohim being. Honestly, can one rightly deny that Jesus is referring to this very incident, "How art thou fallen from heaven, O Lucifer," when in Luke 10:18 he says, "I beheld Satan as lightning fall from heaven"? Beyond the established discussion of the whole context here, it is, then, also evident just from these added underlines of the latter verses that there is a secondary meaning to the Isaiah and Ezekiel scriptures that relates to the personage who has come to be known as the devil himself; and "if" the devil figure is indeed from this "thou hast been in Eden" Pre-Adamic Ezekiel 28:13 **Eden-I** within the timeframe of Genesis 1:1, then so are the people and nations that are also inseparably established there scripturally.

Interestingly, but not surprisingly, Pre-Adamic humanoid remains have been discovered, dating back to the last Ice Age ten to twelve thousand years ago, discovered in 1999 at an archaeological dig in Woodburn, Oregon. Human hairs were found perfectly preserved with enough follicles for DNA analysis. Geology professor emeritus William Orr, at the University of Oregon, spoke of DNA analysis efforts to match the Ice Age hair to any living hominid species on earth today, an unsuccessful venture. Advocates of The Darwinian Mythology would prefer to link such evidence with Adamic human genetics, but the unrelated Pre-Adamic race was wiped out.[38]

To reassert the context, hopscotching *within* the transitioned flashbacks (i.e., erroneously going *from* the original Pre-Adamic fall event, *to* then trying to soothe the potentially jarring revelation by unjustifiably importing our Adamic epoch familiarities into that original subject epoch) is not allowed here in what is at least greatly sought to yield a tour nowhere except within exegesis-land

---

[37] See endnote 10 (beginning on page 123) for information about the misnomer of using "Lucifer" as a proper name.
[38] See more of this type of evidence in endnote 13, page 142.

(the "travel brochure" for which is more biblically intact than the often well-intentioned but erroneous brochure of its detractors). Thus, the law of prophetic double-reference comes across as being glaringly in view through these scriptures.

Such Pre-Adamic *national* personalities, then, are understood to be: (1) *humanoids* (who are separately distinguished from those designated as belonging to the heavenly council elohim who are *also* there, and likewise distinguished from the yet historically nonexistent, meaning, *future* Adamic-k ə ā d ā m[39]) and (2) *weakened* during the 1:1 elohim contemporary degeneration, composing a second source of scriptural witnesses beside those of Ezekiel 28:13-19. This Ezekiel/Isaiah/Psalms-82 elohim connection is indeed in the first version of Eden, an Eden that is obviously *not* so-characterized in the future population-of-two Adam's Eden (who are expelled from their comparatively miniscule planetary-*section* Eden before, probably long before, Eve's gestation period yielded any child); and thus, since these Isaiah 14:12 "nations" and Ezekiel 28:19's "people" are not in Adam's Eden, then there is just as certainly a well-developed society occupying the original (1:1) *planetary*-wide Eden, or to again put it colloquially: "Eden-I," a name that no doubt describes a previously mentioned-in-passing Revelation 21:1 type of definitively *dry earth without seas* (unlike 1:2), thus, the destined idyllic whole-world-paradise that God will *return* the earth to someday. The truth that a planetary-wide perfect world without seas is the endgame world that will forever exist in the "new heavens, new earth, and new Jerusalem" realm of the distant and destined eschatological future paints another "original" picture of the world that is instantaneously called into being as the original ideal in Genesis 1:1 when *also* (meaning, as shall be in the 21:1 new earth) there is no sin, the flawless world that God has always envisioned to roll out his eternal *plans that* notoriously "*change not.*"

---

[39] Recall this Hebrew term's usage from page12.

5

THE THREE EPOCHS OF ETERNITY

That inhabited 1:1 world is the subject of the "before and after" effects of the biblical expression, "Thou wast perfect in thy ways from the day that thou wast created, till iniquity was found in thee" (Ezekiel 28:15). In this vein, then, we see not the king of Tyrus (or that of Babylon) in the primeval **Eden-I**, but the germ-seed elohim heavenly council member along with the other discussed inhabitants who were, of course, not in Adam's **Eden-II** later-prepared probationary and cordoned-off tiny *section* of the earth's real estate that nevertheless retains the hopeful namesake as a prophetic clue about the Revelation 21:1 **Eden-III** eventuality.[40] As God's whole to-be-discussed biblical plan for the redemption of mankind traces back to the blood covenant initiated in Adam's Eden, foreshadowing the ultimate spiritual-reversal smackdown,[41] so also Adam's Eden-II namesake itself speaks redemptively of such inevitable things to come (in 21:1). Now, we will return to the next step in our timeline, Genesis 1:2, the conditions that result from the later and sinful part of the 1:1-associated history.

However, "thereby hangs a tale," an observation that has already been intimated by a disagreement between those who do, and those who do not, recognize the differences between how God produces 1:1 in the beginning, and how God produces 1:3-31 much later. Those who do not recognize these distinctly different timeframes as such, therefore produce ironic and hypocritical rejection(s) of the conventional "gap theory."

Such rejection is ironic and at least somewhat hypocritical because, in truth, the strongest advocates of *rejecting* "the gap theory" also believe in versions of absolutely nothing less than a gap theory, except that such "rejectors" believe in gaps that don't make as much exegetic sense as this study conveys about that topic. For example, consider the ironic position of the (for genuinely good reasons) well-respected Dr. Michael Heiser: "There isn't a single verse in the entirety of Scripture

---

[40] The smallness of Adam's geographically defined Eden section within the much greater bounds of the whole planet is availed in Genesis 2:8-14.

[41] The blood-covenant-based plan of redemption for the Adamic race is discussed farther along when its appearance relative to the timeline's history emerges.

that tells us the original rebel sinned before the episode of Genesis 3."[42] Valid, and thus different, Heiser perspectives notwithstanding (including, for example, the valid idea that there is no ironclad exegetic justification for concluding that the identity of "the original rebel," the Genesis 3 rebel, and the Job 1 rebel are the same heavenly council elohim member), to believe that there is no elohim sin or fall before Genesis 3—which *begins* with a lying serpent figure in its first verse—one must then incontrovertibly, *and self-admittedly* (!), *believe* in a gap, a story overlay place where something could be inserted to explain how the referred-to originally holy elohim-being *became* evil, or even something more about the circumstances of *when* he became evil. Of course (!) "the secret things belong unto the Lord our God: but those things which are revealed belong unto us and to our children for ever..." (Deuteronomy 29:29), but one must understand that the "secret things" and "things which are revealed" elements apply just as much to so-called conventional gap theory proponents as they apply to alternate gap theory proponents who aren't inclined to readily admit to believing in the gaps that they believe in (even if they are not inclined to exegetically demonstrate why they believe in the particular original elohim fall timing of their own non-admitted gap theory).

THE 3:1 GAP?

Are readers to believe that the Genesis 3:1 serpent figure is one moment (at the undisclosed very beginning of 3:1) sin-free, and then (later in the undisclosed storyline of the same verse 1) *transformed* into the lying entity? Is, then, Genesis 3:1 indeed "the history-revealing gap verse" about when the evil figure really racked up "*multitudes* of iniquities" (Ezekiel 28:18 / italics added) before he is "last straw" cast down, apparently bespeaking a very extended span of gap/overlay time when God is restraining the full brunt of his judgment upon this wayward elohim member of his creation, "that old serpent" (Revelation 20:2), availing some space to repent, as we see is typical for God in so many biblical instances?[43] Obviously, since the inescapable truth of the existence of a multitude of iniquities is recognized as being committed by the notorious figure, God certainly *did*

---

[42] In Demons: What the Bible Really Says about the Powers of Darkness, Lexham Press, 2020, page 243.

[43] For a discussion about this way of God that offers extended margins for repentance, see the *fifth* dispensation of The Five Pre-Genesis-1:2 Dispensations in endnote 11, page 125 (the *fifth* dispensation beginning on page 133). Using the argument that the original rebel uniquely sinned on his own—*without any outside evil trying to deceive him*—as an excuse to believe that (unlike humans who therefore better deserve a merciful margin in which to repent) the original rebel was still perfect in proximity to when Adam was created, and then did fall and get judged **suddenly** (as in, all such matters being confined to the time of 3:1 or close to it), ignores the fact that indeed "multitudes of iniquities" are committed by the original rebel in the Pre-Adamic context of not being cast down **yet** (Ezekiel 28:18); thus, initially, even the being who would come to be known as the satan figure is granted a significant span of time to repent.

not suddenly pounce his full wrath upon the being in the moment of the being's *first* of many more iniquities to come. Can I get a witness, here? Now, which gap/overlay placement for this biblically *necessary* epoch of history wherein the truly original fall took place (either in 1:1 *or* in 3:1-associated timeframes) makes more exegetic sense, and which one bears more earmarks of a concocted and imposed fiction-of-blind-assumption?[44]

Fortunately, as if the thrust of the above truths are not enough, the previously alluded-to, but not yet fully quoted, Isaiah 45:18's text runs up the exegetic score (which, thankfully, seems to happen an awful lot with regard to this "beginnings" topic): "For thus saith the Lord that created the heavens; God himself that formed the earth and made it; he hath established it, he created it not *in vain* [i.e., quite specifically, *not* in a *tohu* way, as the recommended interlinear source verifies], he formed it to be inhabited: I *am* the Lord; and *there is* none else" (underlines, italics, and brackets, all added). Both of the "created" usages in that verse reflect supernatural and sudden "he spake, and it was" work, obviously expounding upon God's accomplishment in Genesis 1:1.

Most pertinent here, though: *This verse explicitly points out that God did not create the product of the Genesis 1:1 heavens and earth in an "in vain" tohu way; yes, the very same Hebrew word in Isaiah 45:18 that is used to overtly inform us about a means that God did not use in Genesis 1:1 necessitates that Genesis 1:2's scripturally unquestionable tohu world* [look it up interlineally] *is not expounding upon the Genesis 1:1 sudden creation condition of perfection that occurs long before, thus also irrevocably and all too predictably corroborating the to-be-discussed Targum Onkelos' ancient Hebrew usage of the "devastated earth" along with its discussed "But hayah became" features of Genesis 1:2.*

THE BIBLE IS NOT A THEORY

Did God "he spake, and it was" create the 1:1 earth in *a devastated condition* that causes holy sin-free elohim shouts of apparently *perverse* destruction-fetish joy? Of course not. "If" indeed not, as Psalms 33:6 & 9 (et al.) says, then it becomes devastated by the time of 1:2 just as God's word so perspicuously and repeatedly indicates. The perfect and complete 1:1 world did not become subject to God's divine "give'm the ol' 1:2" devastation before it was perfect and Isaiah 45:18

---

[44] Not being one to cower from an honorable challenge, the thrown-down gauntlet of those who reject the so-called "gap theory," essentially daring their "opponents" to present, as they do, what many would consider to be "way out there" forms of extrabiblical support rationale for favored positions, see endnote 12, page 138, for a genuine Near-Death-Experience heavenly visitation that, through direct testimony of an understatedly interesting Personage of that realm, supports the timeframe of "the gap theory."

inhabited, for judgment is levied only upon free agent being contexts, not upon inanimate and disorganized space-time-matter elements as they supposedly exist when they leave the Creator's hand (a secondary-assumption-infused conjecture that many classic-gap-theory deniers believe about the entire 1:1 condition). Of course, this also supports the Bible's exegetically corroborated point about associated 1:1 populations also coming under judgment long before the time of Adam. Once the truly "in vain / tohu" world of 1:2 does initially manifest, the earth lies in that dormant state of "The Fall of the House of Usher" waste for some scripturally undisclosed span of time. At some point, though, relatively long after the devastation occurs, there is a 1:3-31 renovation of the earth. It is not a theory; indeed, then, *the Bible* is not a theory.

Unlike the sudden calling-into-being that is seen at the beginning moment of the 1:1 earth epoch, the devastated earth is subject to the spoken-of six 24-hour perimeter of "And God said…and the evening and the morning were the…[variously numbered] day" stages composed of ongoing corrective activity starting on day 1 of 1:3 and continuing to its completion on day 6 of Genesis 1:31.[45] Any attempt to gag the biblical truth about the instantaneousness of the "he spake, and it was" phenomenon of Psalms and other discussed scriptures, by way of the ridiculous claim that the six days of Genesis, beginning with "Let there be light," is *how* God "spake, and it [the totality] was," is grossly misrepresenting God's word, most likely unintentionally, as far as the strictly human side of the controversy is concerned…thankfully, a forgivable (although consequential[46]) error.

THE KNOWLEDGE OF EVIL

Before moving on, let us consider yet one more scriptural pearl along the exegetic chain revealing the realities of the Pre-Adamic world that have been established. We know that in the Pre-Adamic Eden, evil already exists in the universe, as evinced by the "thou hast sinned" historical correlation of Ezekiel 28:16 and by the so-related Genesis 1:2 devastation…*and* now, by the already present tree of THE KNOWLEDGE OF good and EVIL before the time of Genesis 3:1. In the context of Genesis 2:9's part of the *elaboration* about such day 3 fruit trees, the tree of knowledge of good and evil is

---

[45] The reason 1:1 is instant, whereas 1:3 and beyond are not instant, is addressed in the main text, farther along in the timeline.

[46] Accuracy in "beginning matters" is evangelically important; for example, the wolfishly false and thus surpassingly unnecessary teaching that the cosmic totality is about 6000 years old is enough to drive many people away from the rest of the biblical message. This is NOT referring to the equally bad practice of trying to make the Bible fit into The Darwinian Mythology, for that would be changing the subject, speaking untruth, etc. The simple truth of the matter is that, irrespective of the longer timeframes associated with The Darwinian Mythology, the Bible doesn't teach that the cosmic totality is only about 6000 years old; only Adam's epoch is about 6000 years old.

first mentioned by name. Adam isn't created until day 6. Knowledge of evil—and not secondary-assumptively-referring to God's omniscience including his knowing that evil will exist only in the Adamic future—exists before Adam is created. There is no indication in the scriptures for believing that the tree of knowledge of good and evil is made at any time other than when all the other fruit trees are made on day 3 (in Genesis 1:11-12), obviously primarily including those that are in the special garden made for Adam's probationary beginning (i.e., the cordoned-off or separated garden being within the broader context of a far less appealing planetary-wide environment, apparently a gated community when the 3:24 east side is considered, stimulating one to wonder about the purpose of gates and fences).

In that introductory Genesis 2 *recap* part, thus using some Genesis 1 elements (including a non-1:1 summative reference to 1:3-31's making the heavens and earth function properly again in consideration of the 1:2 devastation, and thus making plants, herbs, trees, etc.), we learn what God does with the portion of perfected renovation that Adam and Eve are given in Genesis 1:26-31. And to reiterate that Genesis 2:1 is not referring to the Genesis 1:1 sudden calling-into-being, but to the six-day process work of 1:3-31, note that Genesis 2:1's "the heavens and the earth were *finished*" is not the way to describe a "he spake, and it was" instantaneously and originally "*begun and* finished" phenomenon, but one that necessitates a process that must indeed become "finished" over the course of the six days. This is precisely why the Genesis 2:4 recap element informs us not only that "These are the generations [plural form] of the heavens and of the earth when they were created [thus originally created in 1:1—the First Generation]...," but also that: "...in the day that the Lord God made the earth and the heavens [thus subsequently renovated in 1:3 and beyond—the Second Generation]" fully operational again (brackets added). There is a very good reason why exegesis demands that more than a single generation of heavens and earth exist by the time of Genesis 2:4; it boggles an exegetically inclined mind when fellow confessing Christians manifest effects of being influenced to *fail* to recognize this "generations plurality" truth along with its host of biblical corroborations. This isn't the first time when such unbelief is biblically marveled at (Mark 6:6).

Regarding those who wish to deny the 1:1-2 gap overlay necessity, perhaps they would be interested in, besides adding their discussed 3:1-proximity gap overlay story speculation (or alternately, placing a gap anywhere besides where it is supposed to be—*which is in the 1:1-2 timeframe*), also adding yet another gap overlay to Genesis 2. That way, it could be further baselessly speculated that God *didn't* create all the fruit trees at the time of Genesis 1:11-12 (which rightly places "the knowledge of...evil" ever closer to 1:1-2 where it belongs, being its origin), but had a (nonbiblical) second round of fruit-tree-making in Genesis 2. But then, if so, that proposed second-round action would have to be carried out as if to hide said action by means of (besides by *not saying so*) including it—that is, by *camouflaging it* for whatever "reason"—within the very context of multiple chapter 2 *recap* elements, necessitating that only *the* notorious fruit tree *wasn't* part of the recap. To quote a great precedent philosopher, "C'mon, man."

Lastly, here, the 1:31 declaration that everything God made is very good refers to the wonderful renovation itself, in response to the 1:2 devastation, and not to everything that is ever previously made, and not to everything that ever previously occurs in the cosmic totality. So 1:2 isn't good, and the six days' *day 2*, being the only day of the six that is not declared to be good, isn't good either; most likely, that's because day 2 is the day when the atmosphere/firmament is made, which apparently becomes the home-environment for the fallen elohim who are yet in the vicinity, the infamous "prince of the power of the air" (Ephesians 2:2) and company, thus lending further credence to the idea that God's 1:31 declaration is quite selectively referring to the renovation progression itself, and not to the numerous extant evidentiary things that are antagonistic to it. The clear overreach, then, of the attempt to make the 1:31 "very good" apply to the 1:1-2 history, and to the uniquely "not declared 'good'" day 2, speaks to the weak case "evidence" for the denial of the better gap overlay exegesis that has been the subject of this study so far.

6

EPOCHAL ELABORATION

As established in the previous chapter, the Genesis 1:1 perfect world, with its Pre-Adamic life forms, and ending in the 1:2 devastation, is the first of the three great epochs in the unfolding of eternal history.[47] The second great epoch, otherwise known as our present The Adamic Epoch (or Age), occurs from the time of Genesis 1:3 through Revelation 20:15; the third being from Revelation 21:1 and beyond. Thus, Genesis 1:1 is a complete and perfect cosmic creation including: (1) *God*, (2) innumerable lesser Pre-Adamic *elohim* heavenly council members, and (3) the Pre-Adamic people and nations of Isaiah 14 and Ezekiel 28 (amid all other present life forms unspecified here, including animals, for example, as intimated in footnote 47). All three element types, present within each great epoch, amount to what could be called a tripartite world order.

This "God, elohim, human-type" order exists in all three. Never was there a completely established epoch, and never will there be a completely established epoch, wherein any of these three elements are absent. The first epoch serves as a template, or a form of mirror, for the other two; for example, as we have already seen, the ideal world without seas of Revelation 21:1 casts light upon the existence of the ideal, perfect, and complete "dry ground earth" world of Genesis 1:1,[48] and, in various ways, interchangeably so for each epoch of the three. This is not some independent doctrine; as true for "all things Bible," the legitimacy of each claim must be consistent with exegetically understood revelation.

Another epochal mirroring example occurs with the Bible's two corresponding "1:1" locations: (1) in Genesis—conveying The Pre-Adamic Epoch, and (2) in John—conveying The Adamic Epoch, each such "In the beginning…" usage introducing God as the Creator of all things, the latter book specifying the New Testament revelation of the Word [Jesus] as God, and then in each book's case there is a subsequent great leap forward in time.

---

[47] For a look at the Pre-Adamic Eden-I life forms and related items, see Endnote 13, page 142.

[48] The existence of the Genesis 1:2 devastated, and flooded world is consistent with the view of the existence of the Genesis 1:1 world's figurative doppelganger, the Revelation 21:1-*like* world, neither of the latter two timeline endcaps having any such flood of water.

In Genesis, the "transversal" leap from 1:1 to 1:5 encompasses the whole Pre-Adamic Age and its dark 1:2 fate, on to God's "Let there be light" initiation of renovation work (in verses 3-5) for the coming Adamic Age, such work's natural "Day" light not only overcoming the 1:2 darkness ultimately caused by primordial sin, but also bringing a new beginning for the coming world. In John, the leap from 1:1 to 1:6 encompasses The Pre-Adamic Age to the forerunner ministry of John the Baptist, his associated conveyance of the evangelical light of verses 4-5 only-*somewhat*-figuratively paralleling the 1:2 darkness of Genesis being lit in 1:3-5, commencing a new beginning in both cases—in Genesis a new Adamic beginning from a previous epoch of sin; in John a new "light of men" beginning from a previous condition of men in an un-comprehended state of spiritual darkness; surely, for both cases, in the hope "…as unto a light that shineth in a dark place, until the day dawn and the day star arise in your hearts" (II Peter 1:19); indeed, as in "These are the generations of [insert name of spiritually reborn subject person]…when God [1] *created* him (spiritually and physically *before* being in the womb, and *in* the womb), and then [2] *made* him" (i.e., renovated/*quickened* him via his spiritual rebirth. Brackets and parenthesis added).[49] Perhaps readers can identify other such biblically legitimate epochal instances of mirroring.

BUCKING 1:2 HEADS

Before we discussed the latter "thereby hangs a tale" acknowledgement about those who baselessly reject the Bible's "classic" gap teaching, we were about to expound upon the Genesis 1:2 condition that results from the later, sinful part of the 1:1 associated history. As an introduction to that topic, consider two classic disagreeing perspectives about how the original Hebrew scriptures should be interpreted, both perspectives couched as scholarly (i.e., linguistic root) conveyances:

<u>First Sample of Genesis 1:2 Interpretation</u>

1:2a says, "And the earth | was without form, | and void…"
In Hebrew: *Vav Erets*　　|　*hayah tohu*　　|　*bohu*

The Hebrew word for 1:2a's "was," *hayah*, is the same
word used in Genesis 2:7 where man *hayah*-became a

---

[49] A couple of things here; first, as intimated on page 12's footnote 23, such terms as "man," "mankind," and thus as in such above universal "him" usages, etc., refer equally to all those who have emerged from Adam, male and female. Second, "Before I formed thee in the belly I knew thee; and before thou camest forth out of the womb, I sanctified thee" (Jeremiah 1:5) corroborates the above *before* and *in* realities of God's way with all individuals, as he has "no respect of persons" (Romans 2:11); thus, what he does for one, he avails for all.

living soul, and used in Genesis 19:26 where Lot's
wife "was / *hayah*" turned into [became] a pillar of salt;
thus, not merely descriptive, but active (i.e., there was a
change from what existed before). Also, "*Vav*" can be
read as "but" when the context merits, as the Septuagint
(written in first century Koine Greek) thereby deems as
being fully legitimate for its 1:2 usage. Thus, Genesis 1:2
can, or rather should, be read as, "But [or, however] the
earth became [or 'had become'] without form, and void"
(brackets added).

Second Sample of Genesis 1:2 Interpretation

1:2a says, "And the earth | was without form, | and void…"
In Hebrew: *Vav Erets* | *hayah tohu* | *bohu*

"*Hayah*" should not be translated as "became" because it is
merely an acceptable secondary meaning (subject to
appropriate context), as opposed to its primary meaning.
Also, when the Hebrew letter "*Vav*" is attached to a noun
phrase, "the earth," the statement is parenthetical, detailing
circumstances as they presently exist, and not indicative of
a "but…became" shift in circumstances. [50]

Many otherwise biblically savvy Christians, believers in the less justifiable latter interpretation, owe their perspectives about how to understand Genesis 1:1-2 to an erroneously conceived war about words. It is clear, then, that an understanding of the Hebrew language is important. Non-Hebrew-origin professors and associated seminaries, commentaries, grammarians, etc., may argue seemingly authoritatively about what a Hebrew expression means, but—to the degree of the modern Hebrew's knowledge of *ancient* Hebrew nuances—such modern literate Hebrews would be less subject to such argumentation.

---

[50] In other words, and to point out only one of many problems for those who ascribe to this belief, such a position denies Genesis 1:1 as occurring in the biblical "He spake, and it was" immediacy. That aberrant denial perspective requires the multi-faceted steps of the **six days** in Genesis 1 to become the explanation about **how** God "spake, and it [all the stars, the heavens of heavens, etc.] was." Mercy.

Of course, the Bible is written in Hebrew, by Hebrews, for Hebrews; unless one has a way to access the culture and language of ancient Hebrew usage, it *has to be admitted* that it is harder to say what the Bible means in certain places, especially since modern people do not typically have the oft-spoken-of *proverbial ancient Hebrew* living inside their heads. Thus, the Hebrews, and then more pertinently the ancient Hebrews, have something as it relates to the scriptures that we (including *contemporary* experts in Hebrew) do *not*—a contemporarily perfect knowledge of the biblical Hebrew language and culture of old. Therein, consider the *Targum Onkelos*.

THE TARGUM ONKELOS

The early 2nd century Jewish Aramaic *Targum Onkelos* is an official translation of the Hebrew Torah; the author is a 1st century man, named Onkelos, a famous convert to Judaism (c. 35–120 AD). And, significantly, to this day in Yemenite Jewish communities, *Targum Onkelos* is recited by heart, along with the Torah, in synagogue as a verse-by-verse translation. Onkelos' translation of the Pentateuch (Five Books of Moses) is almost entirely a word-by-word literal translation of the Hebrew Masoretic Text. However, where there are passages that would be predictably difficult for a non-Hebrew reader to understand properly, Onkelos seeks to clarify these *inevitably-to-be-perceived-as* ambiguities. Onkelos is our ancient equalizer.

An example of such changes made by Onkelos in which he conveys the proper underlying meaning of a verse that would be clearly understood only by original language ancient Hebrew readers is: "And the [obviously already existing, formerly dry] earth was devastated and empty..." (Genesis 1:2a / brackets added). Thus, note that the described circumstances of the earth's condition should not be explained as: an unorganized state that is merely synonymous with or comparable to *only the results of* an environment that has been devastated or destroyed.

Rather, the usage is contextually understood to be a perfect and complete 1:1 / Isaiah 45:18 / Psalms 33:9a / (et al.) earth that, for reasons not mentioned right there, but to be expounded upon within the fulness of the biblical record (which the original Holy Ghost inspired compilers of Genesis didn't even have), necessarily *became* devastated, destroyed, etc. For certainly the universal 1:1 phenomenon that we have discussed is not "he spake, and it was" created as a devastated thing, but as a literally perfect and scintillatingly glorious thing, inspiring rounds of unrestrainable Job 38 elohim joy at the very sight of its zapping into existence.[51] This is because inanimate materials

---

[51] This "zapping into existence" phenomenon is, in principle, comparable to the religiously atheistic Big-Bang-associated occurrence except that the non-empirical initiation source that atheists appeal to (i.e., absolute nonexistence

themselves do not spontaneously manifest the meaning of the term's verb form indicative of action that is synonymously taken to ruin, lay waste, demolish, annihilate, or raze something at or after the fact of creation, and neither does it seem likely that such a speculatively macabre sight would inspire much angelic joy. (Indeed, this 1:2 event isn't intended as a prequel for such homage, say, as John Ruskin's "savageness" in Gothic Architecture conveys.[52]) The meaning of "devastated" is dependent upon something happening (obviously beyond the existence of such inanimate materials) that *causes* devastation. Also keep in mind a key truth of this topic, that "there are as many Hebrew scholars who will adamantly declare that the Hebrew demands the translation 'became' in Genesis 1:2" as the amount of those who have preconceptions compelling them to deny it.[53]

Simply, the revelation demands the existence of free agent beings: the Pre-Adamic elohim heavenly council beings who are eyewitnesses to the Genesis 1:1 perfect creation—beings who are instrumental in that once perfect and complete planet earth, along with all of its discussed inhabitants, later becoming devastated.

The associated words of our above-discussed box-quoted Genesis 1:2 scholarly word-root comparisons, "*tohu*" and "*bahu*" (denoting the devastation), are found together only in two other biblical passages, both of which clearly express *what else* (!) but the ruin caused by an outpouring of the wrath of God. In a prophecy of Isaiah, after a fearful description of the fall of a place called "Idumea," it is declared: "he shall stretch out upon it the line of confusion, and the stones of emptiness" (Isaiah 34:11b). Now, realize well that the English translations there, "confusion" and "emptiness," trace directly to the exact two linguistic elements, in the Hebrew, composing the Genesis 1:2 expression, rendered "without form תֹהוּ and void בְֹהוּ." Who's okay with ignoring that, or worse, with incorporating any manner of secondary-assumption-based 'wannabe' *reversals* about it?

"itself") does not have the one and only biblical God's "ability to get the job done" quality of resumé.

[52] See: John Ruskin's "The Stones of Venice, Vol. 2, Chp. 6 / 'savageness' in Gothic Architecture (1853)."

[53] Thomas O. Lambdin. (1971). Introduction to Biblical Hebrew. Darton, Longman and Todd Ltd. ISBN 978-0-232-51369-1. / Also, Rotherham's Emphasized Bible translates the passage, "Now the earth had become waste..."; the Chaldee Version, "But the earth had become desert and empty"; the Aramaic Version, "And the earth had become ruined and uninhabited"; and the Septuagint Version, "But the earth had become unfurnished and empty." The scholars had biblically and grammatically sound reasons for translating ha-ye-ta as "became" or "become" in Genesis 1:2.

7

JEREMIAH QUOTES 1:2

THERE IS, THEN, *NO POSSIBILITY* OF HONESTLY MISTAKING THE MEANING OF THE WORDS HERE (IN ISAIAH 34 above), and likewise for those in the next passage that we shall presently examine, which are at least as conclusive. For, in describing the devastation of Judah and Jerusalem, Jeremiah literally likens it to the Pre-Adamic destruction itself, in exclaiming, "I beheld the earth, and, lo, it was without form, and void [thus here again, actually *citing* Genesis 1:2]; and the heavens, and they had no light. I beheld the mountains, and, lo they trembled, and all the hills moved lightly. I beheld, and lo, there was no man [i.e., necessarily *not even one*], and all the birds of the heavens were fled. I beheld, and lo, the fruitful place was a wilderness, and all the cities thereof were broken down at the presence of the Lord, and by His fierce anger. For thus hath the Lord said, The whole land shall be desolate; yet will I not make a full end" (Jeremiah 4:23-27 / underline and brackets added).

Some have argued that this refers to the flood in Noah's time, but the parallels are checked by the how-can-it-not-be-divinely-intentional very rare usage of the scripture's (underlined) context-clarifying and epoch-identifying *Genesis 1:2* **quotation**, thus, yet another instance (besides the Ezekeil 28 and Isaiah 14 precedents) of beginning with an Adamic era occurrence (from Jeremiah) that prophetically rises to the point of sharing insight about this work's biblically established primordial significance. Consider the second underlined pair of terms from the scripture above, with the singular Hebrew form of man / אִישׁ. This literally reveals that indeed "no man" survived, *distinguishing* the zero-survivors body-count of Pre-Adamites conclusion via the Genesis 1:2 event, *from* the preserved Adamic seed multiplicity of (eight) survivors of the flood of Noah. Again, this presents another "Are we going to go with what is actually plainly declared here, about 'no man' and thus no remnant to carry on the epoch's heritage?" or are we going to try to apply yet another secondary-assumption-based reversal to it? Since it testifies to the exegetic reality, how about let's just stick with what is said. So the only fully qualifying "Game over, man!" catastrophe is indeed the 1:2 *tohu bahu* catastrophe, but even so, not to bring a complete end; why (?), simply and sensibly because the Adamic race is supplanting the Pre-Adamic race. God is not abandoning his plan that is, albeit incrementally—and come hell or living water!—leading to the Epoch III new heavens, new earth, and new Jerusalem.

Given what has already been biblically established, any further evidence proving that our Genesis 1:2 verse *does not* describe a mere chaotic mass *which God supposedly first created (in 1:1)*, and then very soon afterwards supposedly fashions into 1:3-31 shape (*all* occurring approximately 6000 years ago), though such disproving evidence against such a view is true enough, might really be irritatingly *redundant* to human emotions. Perhaps, then, we should just use the Bible's redundance motif about this topic to *stick it* to nonhuman forces of the cosmos. Let it be so. Therefore, **Notice**: We have already been told that God did not create the earth as a "tohu" event (Isaiah 45:18); remember, *again*, one more time? This "tohu" word, therefore, no matter what rhetorical shenanigans are played with its meaning, cannot be descriptive of the earliest 1:1 condition of earth…"uh," necessitating that the in-real-time-created perfect and complete 1:1 eventually became 1:2 devastated.

THE GEOLOGICAL AGES

There is, therefore, ample space between the last part of the first verse of Genesis 1 and the end of the second verse of Genesis 1 for all the geological ages of the at-that-time *humanly* uninhabited planet (meaning, fallen, immortal elohim could have still been associated with the devastated planetary proximity). There is no biblical hint of the amount of time that passed between the initial judgment and this ruin that lasted until 1:3, but the strata of the earth's crust are altered then, some suddenly (and then to lie in relative dormancy, as with the example of Mt. Saint Helens processes that suddenly deposit strata that are, in their mode of occurrence, indistinguishable from textbook "millions of years strata"[54]) or some more gradually.

There is room for a great length of time between the end of the first through the end of the second verses of the Bible. By the same token, after the instantaneous expansion event of Genesis 1:1 (which leaves merely *apparent* evidence of great age in its wake[55]), **Eden I** may have lasted for only a single-digit amount of thousands of years before the 1:2 devastation, and 1:3 *could have* begun, for example, only a millennium after 1:2, meaning the possibility of a very young earth (except not as young as so-titled "Young Earth Creationists" speculate, who flat-out *erroneously* believe that the Bible teaches that the whole cosmos, including the Earth, is only about 6000 years old).

Since we have no inspired canonical account that precisely describes the geological formations, we are at least somewhat at liberty to believe that they are developed just in the order in which we find

---

[54] For more of the Mt. Saint Helens contribution to science, see endnote 14, page 153.

[55] Recall that it is not contradictory for God to **(1) "he spake, and it was"** Genesis 1:1 into being instantaneously, in an extreme acceleration of time event, and leaving in its wake **(2) apparent markers of great age** that (when evaluated with "a normal flow of time" calculation) "contradict" the instantaneousness, but only by reason of which of **the two true perspectives** the event is evaluated. For further explanation, see endnote 15, page 155.

them, but that would depend on what is meant by "developed," for, recall that the Genesis 1:2 / Job 9 cataclysm does invert many strata:

[5] [God] Which removeth the mountains, and they know
not: which overturneth them in his anger. (brackets added)

[6] Which shaketh the earth out of her place, and the pillars
thereof tremble.

These previously-shared verses are from the event when God seals off the light of the sun and stars, so we are reading of Pre-Adamic times in connection with that epoch's discussed race of beings, overseen by fallen elohim council members, doomed to the 1:2 destruction—disturbing, to say the least, the surface levels of the earth's structure.

To recap, then, we see that God creates the 1:1 heavens and the entire planet Earth perfect and beautiful in the beginning (and not merely a cordoned-off section like Adam's much later Eden-to-be), and that at some subsequent period, how temporally remote we cannot scripturally tell, the earth passes into a 1:2 state of utter desolation and is void of all life, zero humanoid survivors. Not merely had the earth's fruitful places become a wilderness, and all its Pre-Adamic Isaiah 14:17 cities and Ezekiel 28:18 sanctuaries broken down, but the very light of its sun is withdrawn, sealed as it were. The absence of sunlight caused an Ice Age, geologically evidenced at the end of the so-called Tertiary period (i.e., the time of the previously mentioned Ice Age humanoid hair that was archaeologically discovered, found to be quite understandably unrelated to Adamic human genetics).

How long the Ice Age period continued, it is impossible to verify scripturally; but in the scene which the second verse of Genesis places before us we recognize that the ice is no longer there, perhaps due to some buildup of the earth's core-emanating heat, and with other natural forces, renders the whole globe covered with water, on the surface of which the Spirit of God does brood.

THE SIX DAYS OF GENESIS 1 PROPER [56]

On the first day of restoration, God commands light to appear in the context of the already existing subject (flooded) planet, light which did not, however, emanate from the sun, but was possibly electromagnetic. For example, light from the Aurora Borealis could exist even though the sun's

---

[56] This section owes some general inspirational credit to "Gap theory page 2006 Ole Madsen – Design O Madsen Media http://www.creationdays.dk"

light is sealed off from reaching Earth's environment. Only considering natural physics, the sun does emit other forms of energy and particles that do not, in themselves, compose light. Thus, to expound upon this one hypothetical example for principle's sake, the thoroughly natural light in 1:3 may very well have been some form of such day and night aurora modification principle being divinely employed in the first of _two steps_ to restore the solar system's consistency in making the planet habitable again (i.e., the two natural light steps of _day 1_ and _day 4_), rather than positing the light of God's presence, given that this first day's light is the 1:3-5 kind of "Day" light that marks its part in the 24-hour cycles that continue on in perpetuity).

Appropriately, then, the Hebrew word used for the light on day 1 is the masculine noun "**Or**," connoting the unadorned or less specified, simple fact of some "light" (and there might be something to be said about how it is distinguished from the terminology that shall be used for the to-be-discussed different light on day 4). This non-starlight/non-sunlight source of natural illumination is, ultimately, confined to only one side of the earth, because no matter how much light exists then and there, we are told that at the so-ordained time of the day, God divides the light and the darkness, limiting each to only one side of earth, thereby beginning the day and night cyclical phases (which, whatever the specifics of the phenomenon are, inevitably yield, synchronously dovetailing with the unsealing of sunlight proper on the upcoming day 4).

And those who persist in speculating that the light on day 1 is the light of God's presence are left with what should be recognized as growing levels of eisegesis fix-a-mess, such as their necessity of also talking around the issue of the night phase of day 1—necessitating that the proposed light of God's presence becomes a progressively roaming blackout on one side of the spinning planet.

8

LIGHT? NATURALLY.

To make every effort to fish for fairness, though, even if the 1:3 proposed light of God's apparently roving presence (though proposing a belief that espouses something that is not what is actually used to separate days from nights in perpetuity) is understood with the same recognition of God controlling light as he did for the Hebrews during the Egyptian judgment, the argument still falls short in consideration of all the data points that have been shared that exegetically necessitate the realization that, whatever the light source of 1:3's "let there be" incident is, the event is not any form of, or association with, the calling-into-being of natural-light-producing creation, meaning as it was in the far afield 1:1 beginning. Really, then, since Genesis 1:3-31 is correcting the Genesis 1:2 problem that happens to 1:1, God is in 1:3 beginning to restore some of the 1:1 natural light condition with some *like*-natural light.

And then, as for The Day-Age Mythology, what in the world becomes of the declared evening and morning of which each day is said to have consisted? Was each vast geologic age divided into two extremely long periods, one pitch black and the other all light? If so, what becomes of the plants and trees created in day 3? They would have to pass through "half an epoch" of total darkness. Such a comically speculative ordeal would completely destroy all the greenery, perhaps more effectively than the "Agent Orange" defoliant, but the plant life does *not* disappear; rather, it is provided as the food for man and animals when they are created. Why create the plants at all at that time if they are just going to sit there unused, necessitating some unscriptural positing of God using his supernatural power to sustain them in the proposed unnatural or non-conducive environment? "C'mon-Man-II!" the sequel. That type of assumptivism interfaces with hypocritical and mythical illusion gap-rejection turf. We need only substitute the word "age" for "day" in the Mosaic narrative, "For *in* six days [six *ages*?!] the Lord made heaven and earth, the sea, and all that in them *is*, and rested the seventh day [*age*?!]: wherefore the Lord blessed the sabbath day [age?], and hallowed it" (Exodus 20:11), to make it very obvious that the writer conveys no such age-long meaning for each day. "Whatever-it-takes practitioners" of eisegesis, in order to support their presuppositions, are an affront to the simple and direct declarations of God's biblical word.

SECOND DAY

A firmament (atmosphere) phenomenon is established to separate the waters that are to remain where they have been on the planet's surface ever since the 1:2 devastation/flood, which are to be distinguished from the waters that are here newly positioned to form a dense vapor canopy-of-a-sort above,[57] but, also intriguingly, that day's work, as noted earlier, is not pronounced as being good with the usual conclusion: "And God saw that it was good." Why, oh why, is the expression left out *only* in this day 2 case? May not the withholding of God's approval indeed be an indication of the firmament becoming occupied by rebellious elohim who remain in proximity to the earth? As we have seen, the connection of fallen elohim with the atmosphere is more than merely *implied* biblically, "the prince of the power of the air, the spirit [Hebrew, *pneumatos*[58]] that now worketh in the children of disobedience" (Ephesians 2:2 / brackets added). In this day 2 case, the earth's atmosphere might very well have become suddenly inhabited with the so-named 1:2-devastation-instigating elohim "power of the air" beings, and, if so, we don't need be stupefied about why God doesn't pronounce the scene as being "good." What else would be a better answer: forgetfulness, unintentional inconsistency? "I trow not."

THIRD DAY

As established, the dry land is *defined* as "earth" again (as it was so in 1:1, and as Isaiah 45:18's "to be inhabited" *non-tohu*-created usages plainly indicate, i.e., the well-established "he spake, and it was" good-to-go planet itself); God's command is to "let the dry land appear," or more literally, "be seen," and not, "Let it come into existence" (as it did in 1:1, along with everything else in "the heavens and the earth"), which would require extreme eisegesis to reverse the meaning via a

---

[57] This condition is such that those on the planet surface who look up into the atmosphere, which is composed of a relatively heavy upper-atmosphere water component (thus merely *exceeding* the water-percentage of the atmospheric physics that *does also persist in our post-flood epoch*), would not see (Noahic covenant-inaugurated) *rainbows* (i.e., due to the refractive/dispersive physics of such a "below water fish-eye view") in the antediluvian world. Thus, it is an inductively scriptural idea that, given the scriptural fact of the "waters above" in Genesis 1, and correspondingly, that rainbows appear only after Noah's flood, that the same more endowed presence of Genesis 1 "waters above" are lost to the "canopy-depleting" first-rain flood phenomenon timeframe that alters the initial mist-based Genesis 2:5-6 water cycle paradigm.

[58] Root: *Pneuma*, meaning a spirit, used of demons or evil spirits. Considering the air-connection habitat here in day 2, it is interesting that "the spirit" usage of this Ephesians 2:2 citation is being referred to, and therein, *not* referring directly to the same verse's phrase, "the air," which precedes it, presenting a double dose, all usages being linked, though, to the Latin pneumaticus, which is from the Greek pneumatikos, meaning "air," "breath," or "spirit." Thus, "♫♪ *There's something strange* ♫♪..." in the air.

6000-year-old-universe postulation, rather than what it is, a 6000-year-old *Adamic* epoch. This day 3 is simply a reversal of the Onkelos-confirmed devastation that submerges the Pre-Adamic earth. On the same day, the word of God goes forth a second time, and the newly dry soil is covered with vegetation, finally yielding all manner of greenery once again.

FOURTH DAY

The Hebrew word used for the different (than 1:3) kind of light on this day 4 is "**Maor**" (bright light from a celestial body). This latter term is the same as the first (1:3 "**Or**"), but with the so-called *locative* prefix, simply referring to a place where light is *stored*, a light *holder*, thus narrowing the indication down to stars, as opposed to the idea of mere planetary "Or" light (of whatever natural day 1 type of light that the Lord uses). The Scriptures do not say that God creates these light-holders on day 4, only that he makes them (to function properly again in the context of preparing the earth for habitation). They are ex nihilo *created*, as we have seen, in the 1:1 beginning. And so the solar rays, as they are now unsealed, reflect off the moon, refreshingly re-lighting earth's long-darkened night.

But in that passage of Job, we are told that the morning stars are a form of admiring witnesses when God lays the foundation of the earth, and too, there is attendant joy in the mesmerizing shock of its instant calling-into-being (Job 38:4-7 / Genesis 1:1 / Psalms 82 / et al.). Therefore, the stars are pre-existent to this modification work of day 4 when they are being "made" functional again for the purpose which they serve in regard to our Earth. Of course, this does indeed render moot that so-called "point" of controversy about the mentioned meanings of "bara" and "asah"; given exegesis, we rightly accept the scripture's redundantly confirmed meaning that requires the stars' creation in 1:1, long before all the stars are <u>made</u> to function once again relative to the Earth on day 4.

FIFTH DAY

The creative power of God is put forth, and then the waters, heretofore void of living creatures, are commanded to be filled with life. A typical English version, "Let the waters bring forth," is incorrect, the literal rendering being "let the waters swarm with living creatures"; thus, the text does not tell us that creatures are produced (in the Darwinesque mythological sense) *from* the waters. Still more grievously mistranslated, the implication includes that even birds are formed from the water (presenting as competitively sick a notion as birds being evolved from dinosaurs). This would be a direct contradiction of another Genesis 2 (verse 19) recap element, specifying that the birds of 1:21's day 5 are formed of necessarily "dry land" *earth*. The contradiction does not exist in the Hebrew, the exact sense of which is, "And let fowl fly above the earth in the face of the firmament of heaven." Hence, in this verse, birds are merely commanded to appear in their respective elements, with the understanding that they are made or composed of earth, not from or of water.

SIXTH DAY

God creates cattle and other animals, creeping things, including land reptiles, insects, and worms, etc. Thus, sea, land, and air are now filled with life once again (i.e., *after* their kind that was originally in 1:1). Then, last of all, and also on day 6, God creates the seminal head of mankind, Adam. (Again, "mankind" is a direct reference to Adam, so, the term is not to any degree misogynist.[59]) Adam is not created as a fetus, or as a birthed baby, or as a primitive apelike grunting savage, but as a full-grown man already perfect in intellect and knowledge, thus, of course, already capable of sophisticated, communicative speech. His close descendants have such skill in the development of metallurgy, musical instruments, mechanical devices, the building of cities and towers, and Noah's ark, proving that the people of antediluvian times manifest impressive intellectual abilities, and that instead of mankind having evolved upward, he has degenerated downward in so many ways. With the creation of mankind, God pronounces that the holistic accomplishment of the 6 days to be very good, and on day 7 stops from such work.

GENESIS 1-2 HARMONY

Contrary to popular deception, and as previously intimated, there is no real contradiction between Genesis 1 and 2; there are only differences. While chapter 1 summarizes a continuous and thus very orderly revelation of historical highlights—first, creation beginning with the 1:1 cosmic totality, its 1:2 destruction, and then through the week of restoration—chapter 2 is just a supplement, a selective recap, adding details of mankind's creation context that we may better understand his nature, environment, and thus his imminent fall. So in the Genesis 2 account, references are made to works and details of the chapter 1 six days (including the existence of the tree of the knowledge of good and evil, what little birds are made of, etc.) that have already been initiated, though not completely clarified there in chapter 1; they are connections to chapter 2 by way of a contextualized redirect about this emergent and prioritized subject, which is not concerned, for example, with

---

[59] If an individual wrongfully uses such a term, for instance, with an imposed misogynist emphasis or slant, then that is such a person's error, but such terms themselves are true and completely appropriate, although politically/ socially incorrect in wrongfully extremist company.

any strict adherence to the Genesis-1-level of meticulous *order* in which the generations (epochs) of work is accomplished.

From the time before Genesis 1:1, we have proceeded along a path of well-vetted exegesis, leading one to recognize the "he spake, and it was" sudden perfection of 1:1, followed by the "but the earth became" 1:2 devastation, necessitating as historical, prior free agent Isaiah 14 / Ezekiel 28 / Job 9:5-6 / etc. behavior that causes said devastation. We already know that elohim beings exist prior to Genesis 1:1 and therefore during and after Genesis 1:1, for the elohim, some fallen and some remaining holy, are still in existence today. This factually establishes elohim as being Pre-Adamic, does it not? It irrefutably does. And "if" that is true, other biblical details (such as these Isaiah 14 and Ezekiel 28 societies composed of people and nations) have rightly and unforcedly fit in to the story and timeframe that tells the circumstances of the ultimate origin of sin that we have discussed. It is the attempts to *remove* such people and nations from the Isaiah and Ezekiel (et al.) Pre-Adamic fall-contexts that are (not merely speculative, but would be) examples of overt self-willed blindness to this part of *the literal biblical story.*

So, recalling this primary source of ancient native Hebrew linguistic insight, this present study's page 32's *final sentence* in the box quoted "First Sample of Genesis 1:2 Interpretation" should be modified from "But the earth became without form, and void..." to read: "But the earth [of 1:1] became devastated" (brackets added). Apparently for our friend Onkelos, at least in principle, the clarification that Genesis 1:1's Psalms-and-Isaiah-defined[60] perfect earth at the time of creation is subsequently devastated by the time of 1:2 is an all-sufficient provision of understanding. With such a realization, it is merely an incidental concern to get redundant with 1:2's "But the earth became" re-clarification (modified from the "And the earth was" usage), for indeed, that additional reemphasis, besides being a thoroughly legitimate translation in its own right, is also implicitly if not explicitly the unignorable meaning when considering the term that Onkelos (and, as we have seen, *exegesis*) very intentionally, very purposefully assigns before there is ever any so-called gap theory controversy that would need a theoretical third party watchdog to be summoned to render an unbiased verdict.

And Onkelos is, then, the one qualified to be designated as such an unbiased watchdog, for the fact that there is no such existence in his day of "the gap controversy," per se,[61] presents circumstances

---

[60] Psalms 33:6, 9 and 148: 2-5; Isaiah 45:18; etc.

[61] There is, naturally, early evidence (pre-dating the contemporary debate) regarding the primeval gap, just not any such stir of controversy about it as in evidence today. For evidence of the early acknowledgement of the gap existing before "the six days," see endnote 16, page 156.

that compose the very heart of the meaning of "unbiased." Onkelos is simply clarifying the meaning of the verse for non-Hebrews. He has no subversive agenda. His agenda is uncluttered clarity itself. Later in history, when people approach the early verses of Genesis with tradition-and-doctrine-of-man preconceptions, they step away from such ancient Hebrew understanding to support their own nonexegetical interpretive preferences. Incredibly likely, the original author and compilers of Genesis didn't even know or need to know the full story significance of Genesis 1:1-2; for one thing, as noted, they obviously didn't have access to much of this topic-bolstering later canon material that assists in one's holistic understanding.[62] Early Genesis simply (and should be non-controversially) shares the reality of a world that is originally perfect and becoming devastated before going on to describe how God restores the world in 6 days for the new race, the supplanting Adamic race.

---

[62] In consideration of Toledoth and colophon data, "original author" Adam is indeed the first human contributor to Genesis 1...*and beyond*! See endnote 17, page 158, for more discussion about this topic.

THE ANTEDILUVIAN AGE

This "Age" extends from the (1:3-31) restoration of the earth to Noah's flood. It is traditionally divided into two dispensations: I. The Edenic Dispensation and II. The Dispensation of Conscience.

I. THE EDENIC DISPENSATION

This dispensation extends from the creation of Adam to the expulsion from the Garden of Eden. Thus, the restored earth's environment is epitomized in The Garden of Eden, the only *section* of the planet that is, ostensibly, restored to its full primeval (1:1) glory. (The sequel-extravaganza to the previous "Why, oh why?" inquiry is: "If the six days of Genesis 1 are even ballpark close to the relative timeframe when unrestrained Job 38:7 joy bursts forth from the never-yet-fallen elohim, indeed— *Why, oh why, are the perfect garden conditions of Adam's Eden NOT worldwide, and then, **why gated/fenced**?*") How long after Adam is created, and Eve is given to him, we cannot know with precision.

Since Adam, minimally, names the major category types, indeed of all the living creatures that are brought to him, of cattle, fowl, and beasts of the field before he gets Eve, this is referring to more than just a few days; if he names literally all the animals, and depending on the hours of his work-week for this project, even a year wouldn't necessarily be an excessive estimate. Neither are we told with precision how long after Eve is given to Adam before the Genesis 3 temptation and fall, although, as alluded to already, they don't have any children when they fall, and we can certainly assume that they are sexually active and fertile from the start. As to the duration of The Edenic Dispensation after the time when Adam and Eve are together, then, it could have been significantly less than a nine-month gestation period, possibly even on the order of occurring within some measure of weeks.

THE SERPENT

But before moving on, let us give more consideration to the adequately translated, but nevertheless misunderstood "serpent" character of Genesis 3, or, to express the translation in Hebrew, the *nachash* character, which is some of the Dr. Michael Heiser inspired territory that was acknowledged in the front material. The "serpent" translation is based upon the Hebrew noun root letters, "nchsh," which can also be used as a so-called noun alternative, meaning here, then, not as a title or type to help identify the "person, place, or thing" creature, but more adjectivally in the sense of offering a practical *description*.

Consider such another of these subject-related noun-alternatives, in the example of "Tehinnah" being described as a founder of a city, being the "father" of Ir Nahash (as in I Chronicles 4:12), "Ir" being the word for "city," and "Nahash" being the name of the city, and thus, in this masculine singular proper noun usage variation, meaning "the city of a serpent"[63] (i.e., colloquially, the place with the shiny stuff). This at first strange-seeming namesake, then, is the result of the city's reputation as a center for brass/bronze/copper-type smithing, the city's etymology hearkening back to a divine being's shiny quality presence that the Genesis 3 "serpent" emanates, which we shall presently explore further. This "serpent / nachash" is, indeed, a powerful supernatural being, and does not refer to a talking or telepathic or possessed snake, or to any other animal; literally, then, it is a "shining one," one so distinguished among the high-ranking class of Genesis 1:1 fallen elohim from the Eden-I that has lesser-rank elohim present as well, right from the start.

Regarding the serpent's shiny association, then, also consider Daniel 10:6's "His body also was like the beryl, and his face as the appearance of lightning, and his eyes as lamps of fire, and his arms and his feet like in colour to polished brass, and the voice of his words like the voice of a multitude." The Hebrew for the "polished brass/bronze" part of the divine elohim being described in the latter verse is "*nəhoset* qalal" from the root *nechoshet*, again connoting the shiny qualities of the material, and thus, as one may perceive, linguistically tied to our established *nachash*.

Notably, then, in Chaldee, given the linguistic ascent association of the "nachash" terminology, it literally has, in certain geographical and cultural quarters, come to *mean* brass or copper, and of course, specifically *because of* the shiny quality of those metals. We see a biblical example of this Chaldean influence in II Kings 18:4—"He removed the high places, and brake the images, and cut down the groves, and brake in pieces the brasen [bronze] serpent that Moses had made: for unto those days the children of Israel did burn incense to it: and he called it Nehushtan" (brackets added)—where the brass/bronze type of metal that Moses uses to make a staff's top-mounting (in Numbers 21:8) is translated as the name, "Nehushton," the "Nehush-" part correlating directly to the mentioned "nchsh" Hebrew root of *nachash*.

---

[63] Strong's Concordance reference: 5904 renders, "Ir Nachash" as the Judean "city of a serpent."

The Genesis 3 serpent can be better understood also by realizing the same principle of shining applied to the "Saraph(s)" or "Seraphim" elohim forms as in Isaiah 6:2 & 6—"[2] Above it stood the seraphims: each one had six wings; with twain he covered his face, and with twain he covered his feet, and with twain he did fly…" and "[6]…Then flew one of the seraphims unto me, having a live coal in his hand, which he had taken with the tongs from off the altar"—where each "Seraph" usage means "a burning one," as also for the correlating serpents in Numbers 21:6—"And the Lord sent fiery serpents [i.e., the Hebrew: 'has *serapim* han nehasim'] among the people, and they bit the people; and much people of Israel died" (underline and brackets added)—where "fiery / burning" not only connotes light, but the burning sensation and deathly effects of their biting influence. Thus, the linguistic root associations yield "seraph serpents" as the best way to understand these "fiery [and thus shiny] serpent" type usages, all bringing us back to the linguistic foundation, the identity of the Genesis 3 serpent.

So Genesis 3 rightly retains much of its accuracy even in the sense of the reptilian-appearance connection. Daniel 4:13's "watcher" persona[64] also speaks of such creatures: "I saw in the visions of my head upon my bed, and, behold, a watcher and an holy one came down from heaven"—the term sometimes transliterated from the Greek word for "watcher" into the English word *Grigori*, such beings were also referred to in the canonical Septuagint, as well as in the non-canonical I & II Enoch, and in the non-canonical Jubilees. These watchers, as discussed within all these texts, are spoken of as violating their natures by means of having fruitful sex with human woman, thus yielding a race of demigod giants, a reality that Genesis 6:1-4 canonically confirms.

ANOTHER ASIDE

A word about these mentioned non-canonical sources by means of another foreshadowing *aside*, involving the upcoming Genesis 6 event that speaks of angels having sex with these human women. The "aside point" here is that the divinely doled-out *punishment* for this iniquity, for such angels leaving "their own habitation," is not mentioned in Genesis 6 or anywhere else in the Old Testament, deferred as it is to New Testament books of Jude and Peter, Peter specifying the nature of punishment for the sinful elohim as their captivity in hell, literally "Tartarus," and to be bound in chains of darkness until Judgment Day (when they won't be any better off).

---

[64] Besides the King James Version's Daniel 4:13 "watcher" usage, the English Standard Version (ESV) correctly translates with the "watcher" usage in other places in the Bible (i.e., Daniel 4:17 and 23), existences that are corroborated without the specific term when heavenly council elohim, such as in Psalm 82:1-4, are being referred to.

Where might one suppose that Jude and Peter got some of their information from? Did they get their information as they were moved by the Holy Ghost? Most assuredly, yes. Would it be shocking to learn that the Holy Ghost inspired Jude and Peter to quote some information from extant **non**-biblical-canon literary material of their own day to compose that holy writ of their own authorship? A related question: "Is everything that is not literally and specifically already contained within the sixty-six books of the Bible therefore necessarily untrue?" The true answer to that one is an obvious and **non**-blasphemous "No." For an example in principle, consider that "Forty-nine minus forty-nine equals zero" is not in the Bible, but it is true, and so it is with myriads of other truths that are scattered throughout creation. If it makes it into the Bible, it is truthfully inspired by God's Holy Spirit. (For sticklers, such information is true also before it becomes part of the Bible.)

In this regard, then, much of the intertestamental Jewish literary works, such as the above-referred-to I & II Enoch (and Jubilees, etc.), are helpful so-called Second Temple Period works that document the contemporary Mesopotamian worldview context, thus contributing to New Testament authors' worldview—*as so evidenced a la citations from them in their biblically canonical contributions*. If one needs to take a break, to regroup, and to process this, one might do so. Upon one's possible return, one might also consider retaining the principle of truth: "Forty-nine minus forty-nine [still] equals zero."

Thus, according to biblical and non-canonical contemporary sources of authors, the seraphim are supernatural, brilliant beings with some degree of reptilian-like nuances in appearance (denoting why such beings come to be known as serpents in the first place[65]). When referring to those within the class who are not fallen, they are seen as God's throne guardians (Ezekiel 1, 10; Isaiah 6, etc., having three sets of wings each, a face, feet, hands—no belly crawlers or dust-eaters, though). When referring to those same class of particularly high-ranking divine beings who *have* fallen, they have thus become the pagan gods of the to-be-discussed disinherited nations of Old Testament fame, but who are not necessarily of the same elohim sub-group of *lower rank* who are initially *assigned over* the disinherited nations of humans that the Bible teaches about, which shall presently also be further discussed by means of an insight from the guru of the gods-topic, Dr. Michael Heiser.

Dr. Michael Heiser notes that "*n-ch-sh* are also the consonants of a verb. If we changed the vowels to a verbal form (recall that Hebrew originally had no vowels), we would have *nochesh*, which means

---

[65] One must remember that the shiny qualities of some metals that contribute to the etymology of such things as the above-noted city, for example, come after the fact of these Seraphim existences; thus, these serpentine/reptilian creatures are the originating usage for not only "shiny," but for "serpent" as well.

'the diviner.'"[66] Interestingly, the idea here is that, through this verb form, a source of insider-deception forbidden knowledge is being presented; *that*, along with the above-mentioned two other attributes of the nachash reference (i.e., along with the primary noun and adjectival usages), amounts to three elements of consideration availed whereby one may perceive a broader revelation of the nachash brand of elohim that is presented in Genesis 3 (beings, as we shall see, that display godlike civilization-building influence that becomes notorious in the antediluvian world).

Summarily, then, in consideration of the identity of this Genesis 3 rascal-plus, we recognize this shiningly divine elohim form with reptilian features, bipedal, and one who uses his knowledge-advantage/*divination*-qualities to get pliant Eve and Adam to sin, basically, the first notoriously dependable "call them chicken!" con, and to incur the infamous judgment of human mortality, pain, and expulsion. This realization does indeed harken back to the Pre-Adamic work instigated by the Isaiah 14:12 / Ezekiel 28:14 "cherub that covereth" who comes to be known as the Genesis 3:15 satanic serpent figure.

---

[66] Heiser, Michael. *The Unseen Realm*. Lexham Press, 2015, page 87 (ISBN 9781683592716).

10

A TALKING SNAKE?

Now, AS FAR AS BELIEVING THAT THIS GENESIS 3 *NACHASH* IS A TALKING SNAKE BECAUSE OF THE ASSOCIATION with "upon thy belly shalt thou go" (of verse 14), one should realize that the being referred to is a nachash/serpent even *before* causing Adam and Eve to sin, a time when the creature's term of description still necessarily conveys that reptilian quality in the sense of its appearance. And it's not that its limbs are amputated after his fall, and then not that God thus changes the genetics of such a class of beings so that from now on the posterity is reduced to a belly-crawling genetic disposition. Thus, the curious appearance and description aren't even an aspect of the curse that the creature suffers, once fallen. And again, consider that the creature shall be reduced to eating the dust of the ground—something, obviously, that snakes simply don't do.

Most telling, though, is that the to-come literal Messianic *seed of the woman* will conflict with, and defeat, therefore, the like-literal <u>seed of</u> this nachash. There's no "Eve's seed is literal" and "the serpent's seed is figurative (through 'the bad seed of Cain' line)" thing going on in Genesis 3. Just as Eve's seed refers to her genealogical line, so also the nachash seed refers to his genealogical line. And snakes, even if one is to no-pun-intended conceive of a demonically possessed snake, cannot produce seed, or a literal physical offspring to challenge God's 3:15 plan of redemption, which is required in order to qualify as the referent for these scriptures.[67]

To jump ahead with purpose again (to guard against proceeding with a wrong idea about what the real seed of challenge is to Eve's seed), the referred-to evil seed of the Genesis 3 nachash is, however, qualified by the offspring that are introduced in *Genesis 6:1-4*. When this is considered, one may recognize that the serpent's so-called belly-traveling and dust-eating are indeed figuratively **exceptional** descriptions of the Genesis 3 before-during-and-after-*upright* nachash being, conveying the idea, though, of one now suitably abased, cast down to the earth, as it were. If eating dust or such belly-slithering are not literal, as they are not (for no such creature eats dust, for one thing),

---

[67] This snake usage, then, rather than an animal, is more like the figurative reference to "[the rebellious tribe of] Dan shall be a serpent by the way, an adder in the path, that biteth the horse heels, so that his rider shall fall backward" (Genesis 49:17 / brackets added).

and given the broader context that should be considered, we are in view of that already revealed scintillatingly divine being that has some degree of reptilian-like appearance and is in possession of primordially in-depth knowledge and veteran cunning, manifesting such a magnetism of *presence* that overpowers Eve's and Adam's allotment of good sense.

Conclusively, though—this is important, folks—the Genesis 3:15 prophecy is not *completely* fulfilled until "the [human] seed of the woman" (brackets added) reigns with Christ during The Millennial Reign on the earth, *WHEN* "the wolf and the lamb shall feed together, and the lion shall eat straw like the bullock: <u>and dust shall be the serpent's meat</u>" (i.e., the serpent / נָחָשׁ "nahas / nchsh" related Hebrew root of *"nachash"* of Isaiah 65:25 / underline added). *Crucially*, no snake, or any other animal, will be left out of this ultimate release from the Genesis 3 curse in the millennial kingdom; the fact that the so-called "serpent" above (in Isaiah 65:25) *is* left out is the biblical guarantee that it is not a mere animal. At that time when others, including "the Adamic human seed of Eve," are enjoying the direct presence of Christ's full redemptive environment *along with all present varieties of the animal kingdom*, the fallen elohim font—the "thy seed 'serpent'" nachash himself, of Genesis 3:15—will "eat our proverbial in-Christ dust!" This should render to naught all belly-crawling/dust-eating "proofs" that the Genesis 3 "serpent" is a snake (or whatever possessed animal, etc.), recognizing that nothing less than this discussed powerful, upright supernatural elohim creature is before us in that chapter. Sorry, but animals don't talk, not even in the Garden of Eden.[68] ***That*** is why Adam and Eve aren't surprised about speaking to the serpent. For the former *fantasy*, read or see *The Lion, the Witch, and the Wardrobe*, a splendid tale.

RETURN OF THE ARCHONS[69]

This 3:15 celebrated seed reference regarding the availability of complete redemption that alone can reverse all of the consequences of the Adamic fall for every properly receptive member of Adam's posterity is in harmony with the revelation "...for had they ['the princes...,' Hebrew, *archonton* / archons, '...of this world'] known it, they would not have crucified the Lord of glory" (I Corinthians 2:8 / brackets added). In other words, again, that covertly couched promise is offered in 3:15, revealing that someone in "the seed" bloodline of Eve would turn it all around, but not couched with enough specificity that could tip off the archonic leaders of spiritual darkness.

If *people* who hate Jesus, due to envy, self-evil, etc., are acting on their own, they endeavor to kill Jesus in any case, just as any standard bloodlettings occur daily throughout history. It is proposed

---

[68] Animals can be made to talk, as Balam's donkey (Numbers 22:28-30), when it serves God's purposes.

[69] This section title is borrowed from the original Star Trek series episode of the same name.

here that the only wrong-hearted beings who would *refrain* from killing Jesus if such killers truly *knew* that the John 1:1 *Word* himself spells certain Messianic redemption are the fallen elohim. The Apostle Paul refers to such elohim as "principalities, powers, rulers of darkness," etc. They are not people. Of course, the human religious leaders of the Jews and the occupation of the Roman establishment are the contemporarily in-place natural vehicles, veritable pawns (prophetically so), and through whom the crucifixion "of the Lord of glory" is put in motion.

CONNUBIAL ANGELS

Let's further examine this "jump ahead with purpose again" context (begun on page 50) of the Genesis 3:15 "thy seed" nachash challenger to Eve's seed, by considering the question: "Are nachash 'genetics' reproductively compatible with human genetics?" Angels, or elohim in general, do not multiply by procreation, and thus are most likely created en masse prior to 1:1; also, as they never die (unless exceptionally made to do so by God, as in Psalm 82:1-7), there is no necessity for consummating any sort of marriage union among them, as Matthew 22:30 indicates: "For in the resurrection they [people] neither marry, nor are given in marriage, but are as the angels of God in heaven" (brackets added). Marriage is indeed a uniquely human institution to, for one thing, prevent the extinction of the race by death. What Christ teaches is that, as the resurrection would make men and women immortal, as angels/elohim have been from the start, there is no necessary occasion for earthly type *marriage* in heaven.

It is a part of this presently blunt point that however much one may doubt the idea about angels consummating an unholy, unheavenly marriage-type union with human women, and then *that* resulting in procreation (!), the account in Genesis 6 certainly seems to require that it happened exactly as stated; attend:

> [1] And it came to pass, when men began to multiply on the
> face of the earth, and daughters were born unto them,

> [2] That the sons of God [Hebrew, *bəne ha elohim*] saw the
> daughters of men that they were fair; and they took them
> wives of all which they chose. (brackets added)

> [3] And the LORD said, My spirit shall not always strive with
> man, for that he also is flesh: yet his days shall be an hundred
> and twenty years.

[4] There were giants [Hebrew, *han nəpilim* / English, *Nephilim*] in the earth in those days; and also after that, When the sons of God [Hebrew, *bəne ha elohim*] came in unto the daughters of men, and they bare children to them, the same became mighty men which were of old, men of renown. (brackets added)

WHAT IS YOUR WORLDVIEW?

Query: *What* is one supposed to do with that? It depends on one's worldview. If one recognizes the biblical word of God for what it literally proves itself to be, one continues therein. The good Lord gives us these aids, though, for we have only to turn to the Epistles of Jude and Peter for as overt a dual confirmation as the Genesis 6 original proposition: "The angels which kept not their first estate, but left their own habitation, he hath reserved in everlasting chains in darkness unto the judgment of the great day" (Jude 6-7); and "[4] …God spared not the angels that sinned, but cast them down to hell [Tartarus, the worst torment section], and delivered them into chains of darkness, to be reserved unto judgment. [5] And spared not the old world, but saved Noah the eighth person, a preacher of righteousness, bringing in the flood upon the world of the ungodly" (II Peter 2:4-5 / brackets added).

Exegetically, as suggested, the Bible indicates that the Genesis 3 "thy seed" of the *nachash* refers to the *nachash*-human hybrids of Genesis 6, a condition sufficiently noisome to necessitate the flood of Noah, as the latter scripture's context intimates. Would this scenario of the necessity of beginning anew after the Flood make as much sense if the Genesis 3:15 creature was a snake? It is the very influence of the "seed of the nachash," here that very widely infects the human ancestral line— which had yet to yield "the [Messianic] seed of the woman"—necessitating God's preservation of the apparent last uncorrupted vestige of that line by means of killing off all of the infected human family through the flood of Noah.

If one must reel, then "do it with thy might" (Ecclesiastes 9:10b), but in all such reeling, fail not to accept the biblical word of God. The Bible is also clear about the truth that all those who remain aligned with the broad agenda of the fallen *nachash* are "of" the bad seed, for there are some godly descendants from not only the line of Seth, but also from the line of Cain, *but **none** from these nachash. Whether human or otherwise, then, all such rebels will ultimately and consciously attend the same hellish destiny for all eternity. This will suffice for our "jump ahead with purpose again" to clarify the 3:15 seeds of contention, which involves the look ahead to Noah's flood here, as it will also be seen in its rightful dispensation, giving further acknowledgement of that incredible Genesis 6 true story.

Inevitably, then, after the 3:15 promise is given, we read, "Unto Adam and his wife did the Lord God make coats of skins, and clothed them" (Genesis 3:21). God redemptively and rightfully butchered an innocent animal to get the skins, most likely by hand as an object lesson right before the taken-aback eyes of Adam and Eve. The "Lamb of God" whose death on Calvary is also Levitically foreshadowed by the slaying of lambs and other animals is thus introduced with the nakedness of Adam and Eve, save for their bloody garb before being expelled from the Garden of Eden, thus covered in a virtual proclamation of the great truth that, with the only legitimate plan of redemption that exists, sin can thus only be put away by the shedding of blood (Hebrews 9:22).

PART II

FROM THE DISPENSATION OF CONSCIENCE TO THE BEGINNING OF THE NEW JERUSALEM'S ETERNAL FUTURE

11

II. THE DISPENSATION OF CONSCIENCE

THIS SECOND PART OF THE ANTEDILUVIAN AGE (BEGUN ON PAGE 45) EXTENDS FROM ADAM'S AND EVE'S GENESIS 3 expulsion to Noah's flood, and lasts for some 1656 years. Basically, the epoch's title conveys what a member of the fallen Adamic race will do when guided only by personal conscience. In the real sense of this, Adam and Eve had no such conscience before the fall, as conscience operates with a knowledge of good and evil, bits of the puzzle that Adam and Eve did not have until they consumed the fruit of the forbidden tree. Conscience may produce fear and regret, but, in itself, it will not keep anyone from sinning, for conscience imparts no real power to "just say no" to fallen elohim, nor to any other mediation of evil, not even in the sense to resist inhibitions about properly achieving one's spiritual rebirth, which alone has the power to reverse the consequences of the universally inherited Genesis 3 fall for such recipients, thus being crucially necessary for every individual in Adam's ancestral line, lest they tragically wind up paying the penalty for the sin nature on their own in hell.

It is understood that the Lord God explains to Adam and Eve the significance of what would come to be known as the Bible's one and only plan of redemption (to indeed "reverse the consequences of" the introduction of the nature of sin into the world) based upon sacrifice of the innocent, for Abel is documented as carrying on the practice of offering up such a bloody element, a system that becomes formalized in the Jewish tabernacle ceremonies that shall be further commented upon in its segment of this work's unfolding timeline.

WHO IS THE SECOND CHILD OF PARADISE LOST?

Adam's and Eve's first child is indeed Cain, to be Abel's murderer, but it does not follow that Abel is the second child. Most likely, there are many, *many* children born between Cain and Abel, and then in like manner, all the more multitudes as such offspring become participants in the snowballing "be fruitful and multiply" operation, rarely interrupted by anyone's death in this era. Biblically sanctioned intermarriages among the children of the same families are not in any way discouraged or forbidden, or wrong, until well after Noah's flood (at the time of the establishment of Levitical law[70]).

Cain and Abel are not children when Cain kills Abel; given the Bible's genealogical information, one may realize that they are both over 100 years old when the deed is committed. Abel is a "keeper of sheep," that is, his own; thus, he is a grown man. Cain is an agriculturist and also likely the possessor of large holdings. We read that Adam is 130 years old when he begets Seth (Genesis 5:3); Seth is probably born soon after the death of Abel (Genesis 4:25). This makes Abel over 100 years old at his death. The satan nachash figure is not only the spiritual suggester of Abel's murder, he is also the spiritual author (and the not-so-silent partner) of Cain's religion, spoken of by Jude as "the way of Cain" (which, by the way, is not the same as the bad seed of Genesis 3:15[71]), thus the origin of all human religions.[72]

The antediluvian Dispensation of Conscience, then, is a perfectly suited context to host such a beginning for all human religious propensities to the degree of its shared inferior principle: "There is a way which seemeth right unto a man, but the end thereof are the ways of death" (Proverbs 14:12). This era is a time when there is no set standard by which men accused or excused human behavior (Romans 2:15),[73] thus synonymous with just such a spirit of religiosity that would have all manner and forms of devoutness, but not in *the way* that retains the proper exegetic biblical focus, most importantly regarding the proper means of becoming a recipient of God's misunderstood as "so uncool" one and only "I am the way" righteously exclusionary plan of redemption.

---

[70] And even in the Levitical law redirect, the new restriction is not put in place because of any sense of inherent immorality of the previous human-male-with-human-female intermarriage allowance; it simply becomes time to prevent congenital dangers to offspring associated with the narrowing of genetic pools as people groups separate and remain isolated. Once the Levitical law redirect is in in place, though, it is immoral to violate this law of God.

[71] Recall that Genesis 3's "thy seed" is referring to the fallen, formerly heavenly council member nachash seed that opposes "her seed" (i.e., Eve's), and so, "human Cain's line, seed, or way, etc.," is not referring to the genealogical line that will be defeated when the Genesis 3:15 prophecy shall be completely fulfilled (at the time of the Millennial Reign of Christ).

[72] Although "the way of Cain" is demonic in its rejection of the biblical word of God (as manifest in all manner of humanity's religious "traditions and doctrines of man"), that is a different demonic "leg" entirely, compared to the truth that the Genesis 3 "thy seed" opposition to Eve's seed is ancestrally/physically related to the Genesis 6:1-4 offspring event(s) from divine counsel elohim coitus with human women.

[73] We are even told that in that so-called Dispensation of Conscience God "winked at" what he could not and did not overlook in the future legal aspects of The Present Age dispensation (which extends from Noah's flood to *Christ's Second Coming*, which is distinguished from Christ's rapturous *Appearing*, which occurs at least seven years prior to the Second Coming, as the main text shall clarify in its time).

NO EXCUSE

So, as the scriptures teach, they are without excuse if "they" choose to live unrighteously considering biblical standards,[74] for God is very near to even this brood of early mankind, his ways revealed in the passed-down rebuke of Cain (Genesis 4:14) and other evils, and refreshingly, in Enoch's legacy of walking closely with God (Genesis 5:22-24), and in the lesson of God's favor upon Noah (Genesis 6:3), etc. They are therefore not entirely without a knowledge of God, but tragically, they do not rightly invest such potential seeds of redemption, but rather, "they glorified him not" (Romans 1:21), and so, then, God "gave them over to vile affections" (a la the deserved quid pro quo variation of the Romans 1:26 principle).

This realization intersects with the question about the salvation of the so-called heathen who are without the written or spoken Gospel (a position that is irrelevant to all far more accountable ones who have heard the Gospel). If they by nature seek after God, and show by their faith and conduct, according to their degree of light, demonstrating "a Cornelius factor," for instance (as in Act 10:1-6), that in their heart they have received God's redemptive promise, one cannot legitimately say that such individuals will not be saved. But this does not excuse the spirit-reborn Church individuals from obeying God's command about taking the Gospel to everybody.

When Cain flees after murdering Abel, he takes his wife with him. He does not get his wife in the land of Nod; it is merely said that he "knew her" (had sexual intercourse with her) there. Thus, it is in Nod where she conceives and bears a son, Enoch (but not the Enoch of the line of Seth, Jared's son, who is translated alive to heaven). After the birth of Enoch, Cain begins to build a city. Here we have the beginning of the proverbial "life in the big city" with all its attendant evils.

Among the descendants of Cain are Jubal, the inventor of musical instruments, and Tubal-Cain, an instructor of workers in brass and iron. Men in those days used their fallen-nature brains to "progress" in a godless civilization under the tutelage of these civilization-building fallen nachash elohim, and when we recall that in that age such men lived on for nearly 1000 years, besides considering the population explosion itself, their resultantly immense accumulation of

---

[74] Lest one should erroneously conclude from this point (that includes living according to biblical standards) that one can earn a place in heaven by being a good person, the Bible is redundant with corrections to the contrary, as shall unfold farther along in the main text.

knowledge, experience and skill certainly advanced in incredible ways, presenting all the trappings of a distracting civilization.[75]

THE ANTEDILUVIAN ODYSSEYS

The soon-to-be building of such a contemporary ship as that constructed by Noah; the subsequent Tower of Babel; and later the great pyramids, which involve in their construction such a level of knowledge (from divination-enhanced civilization-building influences of the nachash) that most do not rightly ascribe with suitable, though perverse, "credit" to the very first generations of humans, are so many examples of such hasty acquisition of knowledge with its quite questionable fruit. The role of such "diviner" nachash presence in these times is thus a contributing factor, if not most directly so, to the mystery behind much of the posed construction difficulties of these edifices, such as, for example, how the ancients moved so many multi-ton quarried blocks of rock such distances and to such heights and with such precision. It is in the midst of this godless civilization's expansion that the alluded-to startling event occurred: "The sons of God saw the daughters of men that they were fair; and they took them wives of all which they chose" (Genesis 6:2).

This Genesis 6:1-4 debacle is so grievous that the particular elohim sons of God who are involved are not free to raise Cain anymore, as so many other fallen elohim still are, but *these* are those spoken of earlier, those "reserved in everlasting chains in darkness," and are eventually to be cast into the lake of fire, prepared for the Devil and his angels (Matthew 25:41). These angels are indeed the condemned ones for the Genesis 6 sin, the sin of fornication, of going after the "strange flesh" referred to in Jude 7. The "time" of the sin is just prior to Noah's flood (II Peter 2:5). It is the same perverse principle of iniquity that causes the destruction of Sodom and Gomorrah, whose inhabitants demand of Lot the surrender of the two angels that he received into his home, that they might "know them," that is, have not only iniquitous homosexual intercourse with them, but also have such intercourse completely outside of "the bounds of habitation" (II Peter 2:6-8, Jude 7, Genesis 19:5) that directly correlates here to Genesis 6.

The Scriptures at large clearly teach that elohim, including angels, can: (1) assume fleshly bodies and (2) eat and drink with men (as in Genesis 18, when Abraham's divine visitors did eat, and did also warn of God's judgment that Sodom and Gomorah are about to suffer, and did inform Sarah that she would successfully have a supernaturally availed pregnancy with Abraham come-to-term

---

[75] To peruse such interesting ancient findings, see and https://www.thearchaeologist.org/blog/artifacts-that-prove-past-advanced-civilizations-existed and thearchaelogist.org/blog "12 Most Incredible Ancient Artifacts Finds"

in a year), which, for one thing, regarding eating, implicates some form of digestive and/or higher biologic equivalent. So elohim *greater* abilities than humans seem to mean *not* that their abilities are only "beyond" in the completely alien sense, but that such abilities *include* and transcend common human abilities, and apparently with shapeshifter capabilities,[76] thus adding to the list: (3) iniquitously partaking in the human way of marriage with these "daughters of men."

For some, this might seem as unbelievable as that aspect of elohim multidimensionality that enables them to scoot in and out of heavenly and earthly realms. Doubtful "modern brilliance" notwithstanding, elohim are transcendently endowed with the ability to do what the Bible says they do, even without the approval of temporarily unbelieving humans who are yet in their probationary mode of existence. The progeny of this union is a race of giants, "mighty men," "men of renown" (Genesis 6:4). The word translated "giant" is taken to mean the "fallen ones," the infamous "Nephilim"[77] already alluded to. Again, it is clear that those "mighty men" and "men of renown" (gibborim, mighty warriors) were not the ordinary offspring of the daughters of men; otherwise, such life forms would have been common, but they do not appear until this event.

Why? Because these fathering nachash beings are of divine origin, the very ones who provide much of the civilization-building antediluvian "genius" divination knowledge and abilities that has been mentioned. In this truth of cohabitation, upon which the biblical account is based, the inspiration for the tales of yore concerning the gods and demi-gods, the legends of beings who are half-human and half-divine emerge. Thus, the Noah flood outcome of this invasion of the earth by the fallen elohim sons of God wipes out most, if not all, of the life on earth (except perhaps such life as bacteriological, for example, besides the eight in the ark with the animals). Of course, this flood of Noah's day ended The Antediluvian Dispensation.

---

[76] Even glorified latter-fruit humans who will become glorified (like first-fruit Jesus, who, when glorified, "appeared in another form" to his disciples on the road to Emmaus, thus not recognized by them / Mark 16:12), will be able to do likewise, apparently to include such consideration being applicable right down to the level of genetic-compatibility.

[77] More precisely, the "giants" usage (of such other verses as Numbers 13:33) comes from the plural Hebrew term, "nephiylim," itself emerging from the Aramaic noun, "naphiyla," which means "giant" (from Dr. Michael Heiser's The Unseen Realm, page 107).

12

TURNING PAGANISM AROUND

DR. MICHAEL HEISER ADDS AN IMPORTANT INSIGHT:

> Genesis 6:1-4 is a polemic; it is a literary and theological effort to
> undermine the credibility of Mesopotamian gods and other aspects
> of that culture's worldview…The strategy often involves borrowing
> lines and motifs from literature of the target civilization to articulate
> correct theology about Yahweh and to show contempt for other gods.
> Genesis 6:1-4 is a case study in this technique.[78]

Regarding a few example details from some of the associated Mesopotamian literary contribution, it is widely known, for instance, that extrabiblical Mesopotamian literature sports multiple versions of a great Noah-like flood, including a huge ship filled with animals and human survivors; the presence of divine but demonic-being alternatives to nachash, called apkallus, and incredibly, also responsible for demigod offspring from human mothers yielding progeny of one-third human part, and two-thirds apkallu (such as the commonly recognizable Gilgamesh, a giant endowed with antediluvian divination knowledge and associated capabilities of seemingly anachronistic mastery); the Babylonian god Marduk punishing and thus confining apkallus to a region of the underworld, etc.

Not quite incidentally, thus rightfully adding to the above list, is the Mesopotamian literary worldview (of the apkallu) that posits the disembodied spirits of deceased Nephilim and their offspring as the origin of demons, such as become manifest in the Gospel accounts, for example. This makes sense, for instance, not only because these hybrids do not fit into the normal scheme of things (such as humans who die, then going to heaven or hell; and such as some fallen angels being reserved in chains of darkness, or some fallen angels still being "free" to raise havoc for Adamites by battling Gabriel's efforts to bring an answer to prayer, by God's bidding, etc.), but also because the popular belief that the angels who fall become demons, ***doesn't*** make sense. Angels are

---

[78] From <u>The Unseen Realm</u>, page 102.

complete beings, fallen or not. They do not crave to possess hosts, such as people or pigs, etc., as New Testament demons are so reported.[79]

Using the paragraph-before-last example of its latter element's presence (i.e., referring to the apkallus banished to the underworld) in pagan compilations that precede the authorized compilation of the Old Testament canon, and then considered with the above-mentioned fact that the Old Testament itself does not even reveal such details about a punishment that indeed occurred to the "apkallus"/nachash figure(s), *but are included in Peter's and Jude's New Testament revelations*, is unquestionable proof that New Testament writers, who shared such worldview sources with other intertestamental authors, are very cognizant of, and influenced by, such parallel non-canonical accounts that emerge from the reported occurrences of true events.

Again, how did the older pagan compilations of the event(s) precede the infallible Old Testament compilation of the event(s)? The very fact that the pagan versions are put through the finalizing compilation process before the biblical canon is so established proves that the pagan record is based upon *true occurrences* that biblical authors inspirationally repurpose—tweak, as it were, for redemptive, evangelical purposes as suggested (i.e., commensurate with the Dr. Heiser citation about the material's polemic role). This proposed Genesis 6:1-4 evangelical goal to use the Bible's earliest-depicted cultures that are paganized through the Mesopotamian circumstantial influence, capitalizes upon the existence of so-called apkallus as renowned pre-flood gods, masters of civilization-building divination capabilities. The 6:1-4 narrative thus redemptively reformats the Mesopotamian stories, infusing truth, informing readers about which aspects of their narratives are valid, and which are not.

THE ADAMIC WIPEOUT

There really *are* "sons of God" elohim Watchers, the Watchers indeed take human women to become their wives, and yes, there are giant offspring from such sexual unions, quite *literally* demonizing the human genealogy...*but* all of these elements—so ludicrously glamorized by the pagan Mesopotamians, thereby the Watchers being perceived as worthy of honor, of being submitted to, worshipped, of being spiritually evoked, *incanted*—are crashed by the biblical correction: "They [you!] sacrificed to devils, not to God; to gods whom they knew not, to new gods that came newly

---

[79] For a much more in-depth study of such, read Dr. Michael Heiser's, Demons, Lexham Press, Copyright 2020, ISBN: 9781683592891.

up, whom your fathers feared not" (Deuteronomy 32:17 / brackets added). The subsequent Genesis 6: 5-7…

> [5] And God saw that the wickedness of man was great in the earth, and that every imagination of the thoughts of his heart was only evil continually.

> [6] And it repented the LORD that he had made man on the earth, and it grieved him at his heart.

> [7] And the LORD said, I will destroy man whom I have created from the face of the earth; both man, and beast, and the creeping thing, and the fowls of the air; for it repenteth me that I have made them.

…is indeed, as so many Bible students have come to realize, "as much of a conclusion as it is an assessment"; bottom line, the hopelessly elohim-infected world of perverse hybrid presence would have to be wiped out, with only eight apparently non-infected human survivors, meaning Noah's family and the animals preserved in the ark.

AFTER THAT

Verse 4's "and also *after* that" part of the Genesis 6 hybrid procreation event that brought earth's destructive flood thus tethers to the *post*-Noahic flood establishment of notoriously evil Babylon. Babylon's tower/ziggurat is a symbol of perpetuating the difficult-to-resist religious knowledge tendencies that inevitably translate as humanistic opposition to God as so in evidence from the nachash-influenced antediluvian world. Thus, "Babylon" is not just a noun, but an adjective, a counter-metaphor, and then, a *spirit* set to oppose its opposite, ultimately recognized in the spirit of the new Jerusalem, God's eternal city. In Genesis 10, Nimrod is specified (in verses 8-10) as the founder of Babylon, and "out of that land went forth Asshur" (verse 11), transliterated as "Assyria," presenting the two mega-cultures that are destined to oppose the forthcoming children of Judah and Israel.[80]

In Genesis 11:7, as in 1:26, and as proposed for the pre-1:1 declaration (of page 13), God again says, "…let us," another CEO announcement to the heavenly council, this time to "…go down, and there confound their language, that they may not understand one another's speech." Verse 9 reveals the

---

[80] Israel and Judah refer to Israel's northern kingdom and Judah's southern kingdom.

notorious results of this latest "let us" operation: "Therefore is the name of it called Babel; because the Lord did there confound the language of all the earth: and from thence did the Lord scatter them abroad upon the face of all the earth."

This affected humanistic spirit that links the elohim/human hybrids of Genesis 6:1-4 to the "and after that" national emergences by means of the divinely imposed language divisions of Genesis 11:4-9 is seen, respectively, in the 6:4 "men of renown" [i.e., men "...*of the name*," from Hebrew: *sem* / םֵשׁ], with the 11:4's "a name for ourselves" [i.e., from the very same Hebrew: *sem* / םֵשׁ]. Such "come what may" shallowness of self-perception that would want to exalt human reputation, instead of exalting God, is the root cause of the emergent nations of Babel into the world being given over to the auspices of the elohim, as Deuteronomy 32 presents:

> [8] When the Most High divided to the nations their
> inheritance, when he separated the sons of Adam, he
> set the bounds of the people according to the number
> of the children of Israel.

> [9] For the Lord's portion is his people; Jacob is the
> lot of his inheritance.

BIBLICAL FICTION TRANSLATIONS

The Genesis 10 list of nations that emerge is thus redressed here in Deuteronomy 32:8-9, except that there is an easily recognizable mistranslation present. Frankly, "the children of Israel" usage at the end of verse 8 should say, "the sons of God" (as the ESV and NRSV correctly translate), referring to all the Babel-dispersed pagan nations being judgmentally relegated by God away from himself to the lesser heavenly council elohim, who then become national overlords of those dispersing populations. There are already fallen elohim in the cosmos and world, way back from some point later within the Genesis 1:1 timeframe, but Psalm 82 reads as if the particular new batch of "sons of God" elohim that he uses to oversee the many rebellious nations that disperse from Babel fell contemporarily, during The Adamic Age, by means of them not properly rising to the task of such leadership as they should have, for the scriptures indicate that they abused such assigned nationally dispersed populations through forms of grievous injustice being dispensed by the overlord elohim.

Deuteronomy 4:1, 3, 19-20 (with Psalm 82's divine judgment against the elohim context of its verse 8 "all nations") also addresses the reality:

[1] Now therefore hearken, O Israel, unto the statutes and unto the judgments, which I teach you, for to do them, that ye may live, and go in and possess the land which the LORD God of your fathers giveth you…

[3] Your eyes have seen what the LORD did because of Baalpeor: for all the men that followed Baalpeor, the LORD thy God hath destroyed them from among you…

[19] And lest thou lift up thine eyes unto heaven, and when thou seest the sun, and the moon, and the stars, even all the host of heaven, shouldest be driven to worship them, and serve them, which the LORD thy God hath divided unto all nations under the whole heaven.

[20] But the LORD hath taken you, and brought you forth out of the iron furnace, even out of Egypt, to be unto him a people of inheritance, as ye are this day.

Verse 3's "Baalpeor," undoubtedly a nachash-nature pagan god worshipped by Moabites, is such an example of the fallen elohim influence upon Israel.[81] So, due to such widespread pagan rebellion, God disinherits Babel's rebellious people to become the nations of the world. Relatedly, then, to get back to the above-mentioned error of the "sons of Israel" usage, rather than "sons of God," these latter verses (1, 3, 19-20) that expound upon the repercussions of the tower of Babel context (Genesis chapters 10 and 11, Deuteronomy 32, etc.) are addressing matters that take place before Israel becomes a nation—well, even more to the point, that even take place before the time of "*father* (of Israel) *Abraham*." So the erroneous interpretation, "…according to the children of Israel," is not a negative reflection upon the biblical word of God, but upon those "translators" responsible for the error, which is an identifiable, traceable phenomenon, the cornerstone of which is memorialized in the simple fact that the only nations that are given in The Table of the Nations (that Deuteronomy 32: 8 is referring to, and meaning the Genesis 10 "Table") so sensibly predate the, of course, *absent-from-the-Table* nation of Israel. "The (redemptively) bloody national entity didn't even exist yet!" So, obviously, the nations couldn't be divided by them.

"But," one may ask, "why not argue that 32:8 is also a prophetic foreshadowing of Israel? After all, the same foreknowledge-endowed omniscient God who foreshadows that verse 9 Jacob part can also foreshadow the verse 8 'sons of Israel' part. Right?" No. God's foreknowledge and omniscience

---

[81] This Numbers 23-24 story involves the Moabite king Balaak futilely wanting the prophet Balaam to pronounce curses upon Israel.

has nothing to do with the necessity of confining ourselves to the actual product of original Scripture, which must be the determining factor, and which shall be discussed. That is how we can know that the undisputed "Jacob" reference is a legitimate foreshadowing, but the proposed "sons of Israel" is not. Flatly, there is no early textual evidence for the "sons of Israel" usage. The oldest textual evidence is in the Dead Sea Scrolls, which, of course, then uses "sons of God," as also does the Septuagint.

If 32:8 is "sons of Israel," what scriptural worldview contributes to Daniel's (10:12-14, 20-21) elohim-overlord-acknowledging theology of "the prince of the kingdom of Persia," "Michael, one of the chief princes," "the prince of Grecia," "the prince of Javan," featuring Michael the archangel battling the supernatural princes that are opposing his mission from heaven to Daniel? Again, where does Daniel get the "notion" that behind the multiplicity of these national dispersions from Babel there are supernatural-being overlords? He gets it from Deuteronomy 32. When Paul the Apostle quotes the above-shared "sacrificing to devils" topic from Deuteronomy 32:17, he is talking about fallen elohim who set themselves up as civilization-building gods over these dispersed nations (I Corinthians 10:20, Romans 8:37-39, Colossians 1:16, etc.), which the Septuagint translates ("devils") as "demons."[82] Paul gets such Deuteronomy 32:17 knowledge from the 32:8 "sons of God" proper, *original* usage (as opposed to imposed usages from post-New-Testament-canon times). This makes sense only if the *original* "sons of God" is used, rather than the "sons of Israel" imposition of later, "more reasonable" but biblically incongruent times. No doubt, people are used as pawns amid such contexts, but the teaching is biblically irrevocable: "For we wrestle not against flesh and blood, but against principalities, against powers, against the rulers of the darkness of this world, against spiritual wickedness in high places" (Ephesians 6:12).

---

[82] The Old Testament distinction should be understood that Israel wars against armies that are offspring of the Genesis 6 fallen elohim, bloodlines that are not the same as these above-mentioned punished/disinherited nations that God would bless when they accept him.

13

HOW DISTINGUISHED-LOOKING!

THE SCRIPTURAL FACT OF THE POST-BABEL GEOGRAPHICAL ASSIGNMENTS BEING GIVEN TO HEAVENLY COUNCIL elohim, and not given *to Israelites* (!), and the related scriptural fact that such disinherited pagan nations are clearly *distinguished from* God's Deuteronomy 4:19-20 / 32:8-9 inheritance of "Jacob (i.e., nation of Israel)" may also be seen, for example, in:

– I Samuel 26:19 when David is being driven away from, as he puts it, "sharing in the inheritance of Yahweh, saying, 'Go serve other gods!'" Poignantly, this is spoken by David when he is on the run out of Israel due to the threat of Saul. It is understood that to be out of Israel is to be among the pagan nations that are under the auspices of such elohim gods, a situation synonymous with David's cry, "[Am I really to] Go serve other gods!" (brackets added); and in,

– II Kings 5 when Naaman the Syrian travels from his pagan homeland to the Israel interior to find Elisha, as Naaman hopes to receive a healing from leprosy from the resident man of God. When Naaman receives his dramatic healing, he pleads with Elisha that he would be allowed to load up two mules with soil from Israel before he leaves Israel, because, as Naaman puts it, "Your servant will never again bring a burnt offering and sacrifice to other gods, but only to Yahweh." Clearly, Naaman is aware of the common knowledge that the pagan nations are disinherited, under the domain of the now-fallen elohim pagan gods, and therefore, to keep his vow, he needs to take some holy ground with him to properly contextualize all of his future offerings to Yahweh God, being that he will be in Syria.

JACOB'S SO-CALLED 70

Another aspect of this topic is the attempt to relegate the seventy nations listed in the Table of the Nations (of Genesis 10-11) to being another reference to the "sons of Israel" just because Exodus 1:5 refers to Jacob's 70 personal progeny descendants, referring to those who accompany him to

Egypt. This is merely mindless numbers-matching instead of finding out, biblically, that the trek to Egypt includes far more than the amount who are specifically told to us as being *only* Jacob's, this "far more" amount of people who are also of the issue of "Israel" in every sense of the word. Genesis 46:26 says, "All the souls that came with Jacob into Egypt, which came out of his loins, besides Jacob's sons' wives, all the souls were threescore and six [i.e., 66]" (brackets added). This necessitates a significant number of Israelite sojourners to Egypt from Jacob's twelve son's specified "wives," beyond those designated descendants of Jacob himself.

Also consider Genesis 46:27, which says, "With the two sons who had been born to Joseph in Egypt, the members of Jacob's family, which went to Egypt, were seventy in all." This factually establishes the necessity that Jacob's descendants who left with Jacob to begin their trek to Egypt were not seventy; they totaled seventy only when counting the ones who were already in Egypt. But again, the point here is only that the seventy is referring to Jacob's personal line of people.

Contrasting with the knee-jerk fixation upon Jacob's "70" number that is apparently so ripe for cherry picking from some is the 70 "sons of God." Besides correlating to the division of seventy nations of Genesis 10-11, from which the Deuteronomy 32 worldview springs (which recognizes that the pagan nations are judgmentally subjected by God to God's lesser elohim "sons of God," and that the nation of Jacob/Israel is reserved for the Lord), "the sons of God" understanding indeed *fits in* with this broader contextual understanding of Deuteronomy 32, whereas "the sons of Israel" certainly does not.

Indeed, take another look at Deuteronomy 32:8's "sons of God," and its correlation to its subsequent verse 17's "devil...new gods" who are then expounded upon, likening the consequences of such influence to being "of the vine of Sodom and...Gomorrah" (in verse 32), which shall be avenged (verse 35). And then, finally, in verse 43, "His [the Lord's] adversaries" are called out, referring to those evil entities who seduce the Israelites into like-evil responses that the chapter is expounding upon (i.e., the fallen and/or backslidden elohim "sons of God" influence). The Lord vows to his people Israel, despite the wrongfully compliant brouhaha committed by so many of them, that he, God, would "be merciful unto his land and to his people."

If one is going to eliminate the supernatural element from 32:8, preferring the "sons of Israel," how is one to deal with the later 32:43 regarding God's "devil...new god" adversaries who are being *distinguished* there *from* his prone-to-waywardness people Israel? Whereas the fallen elohim "sons of God" usage makes *complete* sense, "sons of Israel" being substituted there, instead of using the original text as discussed, is a celebration of ridiculousness that has to call upon a creative blend of eisegesis "gifting" and an incorporation of secondary assumptions to "fix" (the unfixable).

BOUNDS OF HABITATION

Paul speaks of this distinction between the above-discussed nations of opposition, those posed against Israel itself, painting in broad strokes, saying, "And hath made of one blood all nations of men for to dwell on all the face of the earth, and hath determined the times before appointed, and the bounds of their habitation; That they should seek the Lord, if haply they might feel after him, and find him, though he be not far from every one of us" (Acts 17:26-27). The national "bounds of their habitation" is a reference to the nations that have been so divided since Deuteronomy 32:8-9, repercussions of the Babel debacle, "the times before appointed" being a reference to the vast epoch, "the times of the Gentiles" (of Luke 21:24, extending from Daniel's Babylonian Empire timeframe up to the time of the Millennian Reign of Christ) citations informing readers that not only are the pagan nations disinherited by God, but holistically are on a fixed "days are numbered" prophetic schedule that can end well for all those individuals who indeed "find him."

All of these considerations contribute to a sensible orchestration of biblical information bits that, once one recognizes the spirit of evil that links the Genesis 6:1-4 fallen elohim debacle with God's Genesis 11:1-8 Babel disinheritance event of worldly, non-Israeli nations, crystalizes the latest element in the plan of God, offering that notorious next step of remedy—the call of Abram to begin the Jacobian foreseen new nation, through whom all such worldly nations would be blessed. The Bible's subsequent story featuring such repercussions of this Divine action to dispossess the nations set against Israel is perceivable as a microcosm even within Israel itself, illustrating not only the principle of God's blessing that can be enjoyed through obedience, but of God's thoroughly righteous and ubiquitous condemnation of all-too-familiar humanistic rebelliousness.

Immediately after Babel, God indeed calls Abram for the purpose of making a new people for himself, unsullied by the influence of the elohim of the Babel event's repercussions. As indicated above, though, one should never lose sight of Paul's alluding to that part of the covenant relationship involving the great all-call, the opportunity to enter into the redemptive act of seeking, a meticulously serious *feeling search* to find God that even the disinherited nations can still engage in while such individuals thereof are still in the human probationary phase of *being alive*. Paul's rationale for his own ministry to the Gentiles is that it is God's intention to reclaim the nations so mercifully through their individuals becoming recipients of God's offered plan of this much-needed redemption that may be procured through one's properly expressed repentant faith in the shed blood of Jesus, for "...if ye be Christ's, then are ye Abraham's seed, and heirs according to the promise" (Galatians 3:29).

Paul's theology is no doubt aided through his teacher Gamaliel's understanding of the Old Testament's great battle lines that have thus been established facing off these disinherited nations against Israel, a conflict that runs through the time and space of the post-Babel Old Testament world. These Genesis 6 nephilim and gibborim (introduced on page 61), for instance, thus yield generations of offspring that are enemies of the Israelites, who regularly conflict with such related "and after that" lines as the Anakim giants of Deuteronomy 3 and Numbers 13, and then, later, continuing in the line of the familiar Philistines, who are partially descended from the nephilim, and thereby producing the giant Goliath. The telltale giantism of nephilim blood lines that are peppered throughout the Old Testament testify to this establishment of enmity against the Israelites through the seed of the nachash, as originally prophesied in Genesis 3:15.

THE PATRIARCHAL DISPENSATION

This dispensation extends from the call of Abram to the Exodus from Egypt, a period of 430 years.

After the dispersion from Babel, including the subsequent division of nations to the lesser elohim "sons of God," the descendants of Noah and his sons go the way of the world, becoming idolaters. In this ungodly context, God decides to single out one family and start afresh. Abram, to be renamed "Abraham" by God, is thus chosen. Abraham proves to be a mighty man of faith, but his righteousness is not as impressive in his descendants. Isaac is good, but nothing like father Abraham; and Isaac's son Jacob has some clearly negative issues, which are more pronounced in the twelve sons of Jacob, with the exception of Joseph. Thus, in the short dispensation of only 430 years, all of Abraham's descendants wind up as slaves in Egypt.

THE LEGAL DISPENSATION (OF THE LAW AND PROPHETS)

This dispensation extends from the Egyptian exodus to the birth of Christ.

At the close of the previous dispensation, the children of Israel cry unto God in their Egyptian bondage, and God sends them a deliverer, Moses. Previously, as suggested, God allows man to govern himself through a sense of conscience, but now God begins with Moses to organize "the commonwealth of Israel," establishing laws and regulations along with a tabernacle system that provides centralized worship.[83]

---

[83] For a summary of the essential points undergirding the blood covenant based tabernacle system, see endnote 18, page 159.

This system is to be theocratic, that is, it is God's intention to rule on earth through a representative that he, God himself, would appoint. The first such person is Moses. When Moses dies, he is succeeded by Joshua. After his death, and then by the time of the death of the ancestral elders of Joshua's generation, the Israelites become quite pagan yet again. This obviously causes another of Israel's downfalls, which, to name one side effect, includes getting defeated by their enemies, being as they are *alienated* from God's blessings. When Israel cries out again by reason of such sin-caused hardships, God raises up judges who govern them for about 450 years (Acts 13:20). Then Israel provokes God to give them a king just like "cool" nations have, and Saul is selected and reigns for 40 years. He is followed by David, who is succeeded by his son, Solomon, each of whom also reign 40 years.

At the death of Solomon in 975 BC, the kingdom is divided, Solomon's son Rehoboam getting the two tribes of Judah, and Jeroboam getting the ten tribes of Israel. From this time of division, *Israel* lasts for 254 years before being carried off captive to Assyria in 721 BC, and 115 years later, *Judah* goes into exile to Babylon in 606 BC. In 536 BC, after 70 years' captivity, the Jews return from Babylon. In this time period Daniel's prophetic ministry occurs.

14

A TOUCH OF PROOF

AT THIS POINT IN THE TIMELINE (CIRCA 539 BC), A RESPONSE IS OFFERED WHICH QUALIFIES AS AN ADDRESS OF the early-on concern about "What good would it do to avail a legitimate summary of eternal history if, due to a condition of preconceived unbelief, targeted readers regarded such a proposal as foolishness, and thus prematurely stepped away from the offer?" So here, as it was proposed at the onset of this work, another step along this timeline's purpose is to provide a meaningful touch of proof about its primary source material being historically trustworthy. Thus, the following section does open the opportunity for readers to share in the verification of the fully available knowledge that the Bible is uniquely true among all so-called sacred texts of the world. As indicated in the "Acknowledgements" portion of this work, "Kingdom kudos" are directed to Gavin Finley's endtimepilgrim.org contribution that makes Daniel's 70 weeks prophecy, as well as the related significance of the seven feasts of Israel, more approachable for everybody.

Again, to foreshadow, in the early 30s AD,[84] Jesus says that when Jerusalem is surrounded by armies, those in Judea should depart from it, and those who are dispersed into outside countries should not enter Judea, because it [Jerusalem / Judea] would be made desolate by means of the edge of the sword, that it shall be led away captive into all nations, and thus Jerusalem would be trodden down by the Gentiles until the times of the Gentiles would be fulfilled (Luke 21:20-21, 24).

This prophesied defeat of Jerusalem occurs in 70 AD, when, of course, the vast bulk of Jews are consequently scattered all over the world, remaining thus dispersed until the twentieth century. In 1967, in the Six-Day War, the Jews reoccupy Jerusalem. In Isaiah 11:11-12, God declares that he will set his hand again the second time to recover his outcast people, the Jews, regathering the dispersed of Judah from all over the world. (The first time the Jews lost their land was during their ancient Babylonian captivity.) There has never been any other nation in the world that has regathered, being nationally unified *twice*. *Nineteenth*-century Christians (some of whom wrote books about this, though from that time's perspective, the national regathering was a future fulfillment) were thought

---

[84] I am not sorry, folks, but despite "scholarship" conventions, I cannot bring myself to use "CE" (and such) instead of BC and AD.

of as actually being nutty (surprise, surprise!) for believing in "this ridiculous (*twentieth*-century fulfilled) prophecy." Hopefully, not all such real-world-oblivious scoffers went to their graves in denial of the irrefutable word of God.

Isaiah 66: 8-10 postulates another related ancient prophetic consideration of this matter: "…shall a nation be born at once? For as soon as Zion travailed, she brought forth her children…rejoice ye with Jerusalem…all ye that love her." Prior to the Six-Day War, on May 14, 1948, Israel was indeed reborn in one day, "at once," so miraculously; 6,000,000 Jews had been killed by the Nazis during that same decade. Worldwide sympathy was poured out on them. The United Nations voted, and Israel once again, "against all [human] odds," became a nation as in ancient times.

The biblical account of Daniel the prophet begins as he and other young men from Judah are taken captive by King Nebuchadnezzar of Babylon (Daniel 1:1-4). This first captivity of citizens of Judah in Babylon lasts for 70 years, just as God foretells through the prophet Jeremiah (Jeremiah 25:11). During this time, Daniel serves in prominent positions in the governments of several Babylonian and Medo-Persian rulers, including Nebuchadnezzar, Belshazzar, Darius and Cyrus. In the first year of the reign of Darius (around 539 BC), Daniel addresses the prophecy of Jeremiah that predicts a 70-year captivity of his people (Daniel 9:1-2). The end of Jeremiah's 70-years prophecy is approaching at that time in Daniel's life when he himself is about to receive the 70-weeks prophecy. Or, to put it another way, Daniel 9 contains two important prophecies, the first lasting 70 years and the second covering 70 so-called "weeks."

Daniel wrote the book of Daniel during the sixth century BC; that is a matter of verifiable historical reliability. Because the book of Daniel contains so many detailed prophecies of things that happen centuries later, some revisionist-historian "skeptics" (who are not skeptical of their own less philosophically sound and less historically corroborated secular blind faith) have suggested that it is a fraud, written much later in history, thus a mere post facto counterfeit. Of course, then, what else are cultically secular types to do with such compelling evidence that renders to woodchips their own inferior religious narrative?

DANIEL'S 70-WEEKS PROPHECY

While in prayer, the prophet Daniel is given a timeline of 70 weeks, or *70 sevens*, found in Daniel 9. As Daniel prays, the angel Gabriel appears to him (during the time of the Babylonian captivity) and gives him a vision of Israel's future. In verse 24, Gabriel says, "Seventy sevens are decreed for your people and your holy city." Each of the *sevens* is composed of 360-day biblical year units—beginning with the edict to rebuild Jerusalem; he is told that after 69 of those *sevens*, their Messiah [Jesus Christ] would come. (That the 70 sevens is correctly "interpreted" as *70* 360-day segments, is quite sound considering the latter sentence's historical implications and related scripture truths that shall be explored and clarified in the forthcoming main text.)

The prophecy contains a statement concerning God's six-fold purpose in bringing the prophetic event to pass. Thus, Daniel 9:24 summarily predicts the total eradication of sin and the establishing of righteousness (completing 69 of the 70 weeks of years). The prophecy also indicates what happens (after "the vision and prophecy" is sealed up, meaning delayed for a period, the delay composing the extent of The Church Age) before Jesus *returns* (long after his birth, ministry, death, and resurrection), to complete the by then long-awaited 70th week of years. Of special note about that verse (9:24) is the third in the list of results: "to atone for wickedness."

Question: "Were the parts of this sixth century BC prophecy that relate to their centuries-later correlating events fulfilled?" We will see that from the time that there is a decree to rebuild Jerusalem until the time of Jesus' triumphal entry into Jerusalem on Palm Sunday, show-casing the identity of the one who would accomplish the atonement for sin by his death on the cross that week (Romans 3:25; Hebrews 2:17), exactly "69 sevens"—equaling 483 prophetic years—transpired, thus also marking the beginning of the "sealed-up/delayed" time of The Church Age before the 70th week will be fulfilled.

TO "(B)"

As we examine these prophetic elements, our first point of study involves: (a) the edict of Artaxerxes Longimanus as given to Nehemiah, and its relationship to (b) the appearance of Jesus Christ—the Messiah as Prince on Palm Sunday—as the event occurs during the Hebrew Passover month of Nissan. It will be shown that both distantly separated historical events occur, respectively, in the springtime under the Passover Nissan moon prophetically ascribed.[85] Although the month is known in which the edict is given, the day of the month is not as directly available; however, as we shall see, the precise time of the above-specified "(b)" is available, so the whole segment of time can

---

[85] The biblical connections to the two Nissan moons, related to the 70-weeks prophecy, include: Nehemiah 2:1 ("And it came to pass in the month of Nissan…"), Daniel 9:25 ("…from the going forth of the commandment to restore and rebuild Jerusalem unto the Messiah the Prince shall be seven weeks…," indicative of the edict's "restore/rebuild" prophetic fulfillment as given to Daniel a century earlier), Exodus 12:2-3, etc., correlating to Jesus' crucifixion on the Passover of Nissan 14 (as shall be further established).

be accurately identified simply by backtracking the scripturally availed timespan from the Palm Sunday event that identifies the prophetic fulfillment of Christ being recognized as the Messiah.

So, let us consider the timeline of the already fulfilled 69 weeks: 69 x 7 = 483 biblical (meaning, 360-day lunar-based) years. We continue the calculation of the 69 weeks: 483 x 360 = 173,880 days. 173,880 days ÷ 365.2422 days = 476 years and 25 days (which converts the time to our terrestrial solar years).

In Artaxerxes' 20th year, he issues an edict to give Nehemiah permission to rebuild Jerusalem as a fully functioning city state. This royal edict initiates the 70 weeks prophecy and begins under the Nissan moon of 445 BC. Of course, the terminus of the 69 weeks comes with the referred-to appearance of Messiah the Prince on Palm Sunday, the year and the week of The Passion. There is solid biblical evidence in Luke 3:1-31 that the baptism of Jesus by John comes during the 15th year of the reign of Tiberius Caesar. We also have good historical evidence that the 15th year of Tiberius begins on August 19 of 28 AD (the first year of Tiberius beginning on August 19, 14 AD), so, Jesus would have begun his public ministry in the fall of 28 AD; 3-plus years of ministry later would be 32 AD—Palm Sunday in the spring, during Passover.

CONNECTING THE TWO MOONS

As partially established two paragraphs ago, a curious and wonderful aspect of the timeline of the 69 weeks is that the segment must connect two Nissan moons that are 476 years and 25 days apart. What can we conclude from this necessity of going 25 days beyond the 476 years? Simply that the 69 weeks must terminate in a year that sees a late Nissan Passover. Late Passovers occur in embolismic years, meaning years that require an intercalation of an extra month of Adar into the Hebrew calendar. This 13th month boosts the month of Nissan up in the year to make for a late Passover. There are seven of these embolismic years in the 19-year Jewish calendar cycle. "If" the prophecy of the 69 sevens of years is true and if our calculations are correct, then our timeline must connect into the discussed two Nissan moons (beginning with Artaxerxes' in 445 BC and ending with Palm Sunday's in 32 AD).

This discussed Nissan timespan, terminating in 32 AD, is a long one, with a tally of 5,888 moons (the others being pseudo-viable, having only 5,887 moons). The 69-week timeline of 476 years and 25 days manages to connect two Nissan moons only when it terminates in 32 AD. (Attempts to make the 69-week timeline connect with the Nissan moons in other pseudo-viable ranges of 476-year timespans all overshoot the Nissan moon.) Consider the related rationale.

We concluded that a late Passover is essential to accommodate the 69 weeks. We also know that 32 AD, the year of Palm Sunday, is indeed an embolismic year with a late Nissan. We now have two Nissan moons nailed down, they are 476 years apart, and in years that we have verified as the year of the edict and the year of the Passion. Thus, just with this, we have enough information to lay out a general timeline from the Nissan of Nehemiah in 445 BC to the late Nissan of Palm Sunday in 32 AD.

CARING ENOUGH

This is verifiable history and is consistent with, and thus reflects, the validity of recognizing the word of God as such—adding another reason why it is "of God" to do more than what common practice or convention alone may do with biblical prophecy, such as giving it a cursory read, including the book of Revelation, as in merely reading or skimming over it "to be blessed" (as Revelation 1:3 indicates). People in the first century with access to Daniel's prophecy, along with a chronology of former events and dates in Israel's and the Medo-Persion's history, had plenty of information to do the math to get a fix on the year and season for the terminus of the 69 weeks, that is, if such individuals cared enough about God's word to so diligently "do the math." Issacharian and Berean types care enough (i.e., I Chronicles 12:32, Acts 17:11, etc.).

Even using the Julian year of 365.25 days, their calculations would have been a mere four days off the mark. Careful biblical scholars could have put their finger right on the exact year, 32 AD, and the precise month, Nissan, in the springtime Passover season. With a checked sense of date anticipation, they could have circled a few alternative days on the calendar when they could expect to see their Messiah enter his city Jerusalem on a colt or donkey as prophesied (Zechariah 9:9). Earlier in his ministry, Jesus is moved as if to tears, pining over the fact that the Jews at large miss the mainstay of this "visitation."[86] But we do know that some people did engage in this type of calculation that many missed out on; for 30-some years before the date, such people who care are using this and other scriptural information to learn about the Messiah's birth, meaning "the wise men from the east" and even some of King Herod's advisors.

---

[86] Luke 19:44's destruction upon Israel is due to their failure to recognize their Messiah "on this day,"

15

ASTROPIXELS R US

BUT WE ARE NOT DONE YET. OUR NEXT SUCH CALCULATION TASK IS TO PLACE THE HEBREW MONTH OF NISSAN alongside the correlating Julian solar calendar months of March/April for each of these two events that mark the beginning and end of Daniel's 69 weeks of years. To assist in this process, we will be referring to lunar moon phase data as availed via such websites as, for example, Astropixels. com.[87] Once the date and time of the astronomical new moon of Nissan is located, the next task is to determine which one of the two ensuing sunsets will present the thin crescent of the new moon at a thickness visible to the naked eye, and viewed by two witnesses, as required by the priesthood of Israel. That new moon sighting at sunset marks the first hour of the first day of the first month of Nissan, which is the first month of the Hebrew religious year. The new moon sighting for Nissan will enable the Julian calendar date for Nissan 1 for the year in question to be determined. Then, the Hebrew calendar for Nissan can be placed alongside the Julian calendar for March/April of that year.

Using this method, the Hebrew and Julian calendars for the Nissan Passover moon in the year of the edict can be aligned, as well as the Nissan Passover moon in the year of the Passion. To lay out the timeline of the 476 years and 25 days accurately, then, a Hebrew calendar date from which to start must be established. Can a specific Nissan date for at least one of these two events be pinned down? In the case of the Edict of Artaxerxes, as already suggested, solid historical evidence exists that the Nissan moon crossed the 20th year of Artaxerxes in 445 BC; however, as also acknowledged, the day of the month is not known. Again, though, what about the terminus of the 69 weeks—Palm Sunday of 32 AD?

---

[87] Alternative sites such as this have been sought because http://eclipse.gsfc.nasa.gov/phase/phasecat.html, NASA is *no longer* a sympathetic source for astronomical tables, closed off as it has become for the biblical Christian public with regard to a lot of this evidentiary lunar and eclipse data that rightly tends to validate the politically incorrect recognition of the Bible as being divinely inspired.

Palm Sunday (fulfilling Zechariah 9: 9[88]) came four days before the crucifixion, for according to Jewish Law, the sacrifice (of animals) in memorial of the first Passover in Egypt is to take place on the 14th of Nissan, and eating the sacrifice on the 15th (John 18:28). This correlates to Palm Sunday (Nissan 10 of 32 AD), as it is four days before the Thursday Passover crucifixion (John 18:28).

Understanding the fact that scriptural reckoning for "days" counts *inclusively* (unless the text specifically indicates otherwise), and considering the Feast of Unleavened Bread, which starts Thursday evening at sunset on the day of the crucifixion, the prophesied "third" inclusive day of resurrection refers to the third day of the above-specified feast, which is Sunday. Thus, even if one considers the expression "after [rather than 'on'] the third day" (he rose), it is also better understood, as John clearly avails: (1) that the Jews had not eaten the Passover meal, even though it is the morning after Jesus is arrested (John 18:28), and (2) that the day of the crucifixion is the "Preparation (day) of Passover Week" (Mark 15:42), and (3) that, therefore, Jesus eats the Last Supper meal (on Wednesday evening) one day earlier than the Jews eat the Passover meal (which is on Thursday after sunset), and (4) that Jesus resurrects after (the commencement of—i.e., the inclusivity of) the third day.

THE CRUCIFIXION DAY

According to Matthew 12:40, the First Fruits resurrection of Jesus occurs on the first day of the week, Sunday. Some of the confusion about the day of the week when Jesus is crucified is also due to the fact that all of the gospels agree that there is a rush to get the body of Jesus down from the cross, and to entomb him before sundown because the Sabbath (i.e., Saturday) is near, a piece of information that causes many to assume, then, that the crucifixion must have been on a Friday. However, as is common knowledge among practicing Jews, the day of Passover itself is also a "Sabbath," or rest day, no matter what weekday it falls on. According to Leviticus 23:5-8, the Passover is on the 14th, and the Feast of Unleavened Bread begins on the 15th; these events, then, are back-to-back. Leviticus informs us, "In the <u>fourteenth</u> day of the first month at even is the Lord's Passover, And on the <u>fifteenth</u> day of the same month is the feast of unleavened bread…In the first day ye…shall do no servile work therein. But ye shall offer an offering made by fire unto the Lord seven days…" (23:5-7 / underlines added). The Levitical scripture context overtly specifies that the first day and the last day of the Feast of Unleavened Bread are also Sabbaths, special or "high Sabbath" days.

---

[88] "Rejoice greatly, O Daughter of Zion! Shout, Daughter of Jerusalem! See, your king comes to you, righteous and having salvation, gentle and riding on a donkey, on a colt, the foal of a donkey."

Therefore, the Sabbath that marks the day when the body of Jesus should already be removed from the cross is referring to sundown on the first day of the Feast of Unleavened Bread that year (i.e., necessitating his removal from the cross before sunset on Thursday, the 14th), and not referring to the Friday sunset which commences the weekly Saturday Sabbath.

UNDERSTANDING THE DAYTIMES

Thus, armed with our Hebrew calendar, noting Nissan 10, 32 AD, lunar moon phase data can be used to determine the Roman solar calendar, or April date, for Palm Sunday. This Julian, or April, calendar date for Palm Sunday is thus the starting point. Then, the 476 years and 25 days can be laid out backwards from there. Specifically, the time and date of the astronomical new moon for the month of Nissan in 32 AD is being sought. As the new moon swings out about 9-12 degrees from behind the setting sun, from about 18-24 hours old, one can just begin to make out the thin, waxing crescent of the new moon, the sunlight just beginning to reflect from the right side of the disk as the new moon is viewed in the western sky just after sunset. That first sighting of the new moon marks that evening, that night, and the ensuing day, up until the sunset of the following day, as the first day of that Hebrew month.

Following is a statement from the US naval observatory regarding any first sightings for a new moon phenomenon; they have found that the usual time for a first sighting is when the new moon is, very minimally, 24 hours old:

US Naval Observatory

> Under optimal conditions, the crescent moon can be sighted somewhat less than 15 hours after the astronomical New Moon. Usually, however, it is not seen until it is more than 24 hours old. Often, it is not seen for more than 48 hours…But, despite these advances, we still cannot predict the exact time or geographical location at which the young crescent will first be spotted.

By going to the available online moon phase tables for the first century AD, the lunar data for 32 AD can be located. Remember, by definition, Nissan will be the first moon that comes to fullness after the March 20-21 spring equinox. Specifically, then, the Julian date for the astronomical event of the new moon of Nissan in the Passion year of 32 AD is needed. As can be verified with the available data, the indicative "black moon" is on March 29 at 2000 hours, or 8 PM Coordinated Universal Time (UTC). The previously available NASA new moon times (and other such sources) are given in universal time, in the form of British usage, called Greenwich time. The prime meridian still goes through Greenwich, England, so, when the adjustment for the longitude of Jerusalem is made, it is necessary to add 2 hours and 21 minutes to the universal time that is given in the online tables. In Jerusalem, then, the time of the astronomical new moon for the Passover month of Nissan, in the Passion year of 32 AD, is March 29 at about 10:20 PM.

When is the new moon sighted in Jerusalem to mark Nissan 1 in 32 AD? Well, the new moon is seen in the western sky shortly after sunset, signaling the new day. With the availed data, we see the astronomical new moon as it occurred at 10:20 PM, being only four hours after sunset. The first window of (at least) *potential* opportunity to see the new moon would then have to be the following evening, March 30, at sunset. On that evening of March 30, just after sunset, and just as the new Hebrew day is beginning, the new moon of Nissan is only 20 hours old. Is it likely that the new moon is sighted that evening? Such a proposition would place the event a bit on the early side, but such an appearance would not necessarily be impossible. If it was sighted, then the new Hebrew day just beginning then, at sunset, would have been declared as Nissan 1. Was it indeed sighted that night? If it was sighted, then Nissan 1 of 32 AD would come on March 31.

If Nissan 1 of 32 AD had come on March 31, then Nissan 10, Palm Sunday, would have come 9 days later, on April 9. But at sunset on the night of March 30, with the new moon only 20 hours old, it is barely possible to see such a thin crescent. Likely, then, March 31 would not have been proclaimed as Nissan 1—that day in question would have been reckoned as just another day to be added to the month of Adar. A separate assessment of the new moon data, for Adar 32 AD, indicates that March 31 was, in fact, Adar 30. So, the second and final window for the new moon sighting would have to come after sunset on that following evening of March 31 when the new moon was some 44 hours old.

Under clear skies, the new moon at that time would certainly have been sighted. Even if it were overcast, the discussed month of Adar would already have run out to 30 days. The Hebrew calendar is limited to a maximum of 30 days, so in any case, the new day beginning at sunset would have to be reckoned as the new moon, and that first day of the new Hebrew month would have been declared as Nissan 1.[89]

---

[89] There is a mismatch between our present seven-day week (set in motion at the Council of Nicaea) and the seven-day week of the Hebrew calendar—see "Lunar Cycles and the Hebrew Calendar" at endtimepilgrim.org. For example, the site discusses why the Hillel calendar of 359 AD is slowly drifting off track, thus affecting the modern Hebrew calendar that, therefore, is different from the more accurate calculations that are presented in this study.

Under this second scenario for determining the new moon sighting, the Roman Julian solar calendar date for Nissan 1 is April 1, 32 AD. By this reckoning of Nissan 1 of 32 AD coming on April 1, the aligned calendar then places Nissan 10, Palm Sunday (9 days later), on April 10. Therefore, the terminus of Daniel's 69 weeks being on April 9th or 10th of 32 AD (with the 10th seeming most reasonable) is confidently achieved.

MEASURING BACK

Being thus assured that the starting zone of a two-day period is very trustworthy, the backwards layout of the timeline can begin. This time-window of April 9-10 marks the end of the discussed 173,880-day time period (from page 76). As determined above, this is a timeline of 476 years and 25 days, inclusive. To find the day in which the edict is issued to Nehemiah, one must then measure back 476 years and 24 days, to either March 16th or 17th of 445 BC (with that correspondingly favored 17th). What would be the Hebrew calendar date window for the edict? To identify that, the moon phase tables for the astronomical new moon of the Hebrew month of Nissan for 445 BC must be consulted. Reminder: The month of Nissan is the first moon to come to fullness after the spring or vernal equinox. According to the available online astronomical data, the new moon for that date is on March 13 at 4:10 AM universal time. Yes, Jerusalem being on a line of longitude 35.23 degrees to the east of Greenwich, England, the astronomical new moon time there comes about 2 hours and 20 minutes later than the Greenwich time, necessitating the addition of those times, coming to a 6:30 AM Jerusalem time.

Given the astronomical facts of that 6:30 AM time, one may be quite confident that the new moon would not have been visible on March 13th. At sunset the following evening (March 14, 445 BC), when the new moon is 36 hours old, one can be sure that the new moon would have been sighted, and so the coming day, March 15, would have been declared to be Nissan 1.Thus, using the astronomical new moon data, and being confident that the new moon is seen on March 14, the Hebrew and Julian solar calendars for 445 BC, the year of the edict, can be aligned.

In consideration of the Nissan 10 time-fix on Palm Sunday, the Julian time window of April 9-10 of 32 AD is identified; then, from day 173,880 as the beginning point, and coming back 173,879 days, or, in other words, back 476 years and 24 days, arriving on day 1 in a time window of March 16-17 of 445 BC. To progress, one must then mark out the March 16-17 time window for the edict on the Julian calendar which has been aligned with the Hebrew calendar. Using this data, then, one can proceed to determine the Hebrew Nissan calendar date for the edict of Nehemiah, to find that March 16-17 turns out to be Nissan 2-3 (with a favored Nissan 3). The discovery yields that day

1 for the timeline, the day of the edict, is nestled right inside Nehemiah's month of Nissan. Also, this date occurs early in the month, near the time of the new moon, the traditional time for kings to make their royal decrees—again, no surprise about the biblical framework being so consistent with the natural and verifiable historical picture of the time in question.

The sixty-nine-weeks chronology outlined here is presented within confidence limits of a two-day-max over some 476 years. This window comes from that small (perhaps negligible) degree of uncertainty we encountered as we sought to determine when the new moon would have been sighted for the month of Nissan in the Passion year. This period that composes Daniel's first 69 weeks (to be followed by a delay, during which the revelation is "sealed up," meaning separated from the future 70th week by an intervening span of The Church Age time), leaves the final "seven" yet to be fulfilled (i.e., thus totaling the discussed 483 lunar years, plus the yet-future seven lunar years, fulfilling the total 70 weeks of lunar years, or 490 total lunar years of the prophecy), which is further addressed in the text to come.

Note that this study is based upon documented world history and science, not upon esoteric or ethereal feelings, as the inferior Modern Secular Mythology is. It is mathematically impossible for biblical prophecy to be fulfilled by chance. Nobody made a good guess. Indeed, then, biblical prophecy proves the (God-inspired) aspect of the Bible that "can't be proven."

16

CHRIST'S BIRTHDAY

WHAT IS ANOTHER POINT OF THIS SEEMINGLY ARCANE STUDY? WHY ARE THE FIRST 69 OF THE 70 WEEKS OF Daniel so important? Well, in addition to the fact that such precise and verifiable biblical prophecy can motivate every wise person to *immediately* repent and receive Jesus as Savior and Lord (indeed, why continue to play Russian roulette with the value of one's eternal soul?), we need to also realize that there is a 70th week out there, to be fulfilled in the very near future, the final seven years of this age. So pertinently, then, with the terminus of the 69 weeks established as 32 AD, we also have that very same and dependable end date for the 33 (plus) years of Christ's earthly life mission—which, as a positive consequence, restores interest in the discussion about the year of Christ's birth—another companion key to shed further light on the end of this age, as we shall also now examine (i.e., the popular 4 BC should be replaced by a very late 1 BC date for Christ's birth, for Jesus is crucified at some point during the progression of his 33rd year, not during his *36th* year).

First, consider that Luke and Matthew mention Jesus' birth as occurring during Herod's reign (Luke 1:5; Matthew 2:1). Josephus relates Herod's death to the time of a lunar eclipse, occurring between a fast and Passover.[90] This is generally regarded as a reference to a lunar eclipse in 4 BC. Therefore, it is often said that Jesus is born in 4 BC, but this eclipse is visible only extremely late that night in Judea and is additionally a minor and only partial eclipse.

There is no lunar eclipse visible in Judea thereafter until two occur in 1 BC—the December 29th one being most qualified for visibility and remembrance, the moon having risen at 53%, its most visible aspect being over by 6 pm, making it the most likely of the eclipses to have been noted and commented on. Quite interestingly, this would place Herod's death—and Jesus' birth—right at the turn of the established "AD" era.[91] Apparently, the much-maligned monk who calculated the

---

[90] See Jewish Antiquities 17.6.4 and 17.9.3, and Queries & Comments [Q&C], "When Was Jesus Born?" Biblical Archaeology Review (BAR), referring to: "Strata, BAR, July/August 2013" and Q&C, BAR, January/February 2014.
[91] Of course, this refers to what secular revisionist indoctrinates prefer to call "the common era" (or "c.e.").

change of era centuries later, thus posthumously "corrected" with the touted 4 BC date, was not so far off as has been supposed.[92]

Part of the discussions about the proposed death of Herod in 4 BC (used for determining the date of Jesus' birth) also relates to a few short statements by Josephus about the lengths of reigns of Herod's sons. Given the explicit statements of Josephus about the authority and honor Herod granted to his sons during the last years of his life, it is understandable why all three of his successors most likely decide to antedate their reigns to the time when they are granted these measures of royal authority while their father is still alive. Although they are not officially recognized by the Roman government until after Herod's death, they nevertheless appear to have reckoned their reigns from about 4 BC.[93] This historical information, including the former data of Jesus being in his 33rd year at the time of his crucifixion, and prophetically coinciding with the terminus of Daniel's 69 weeks in 32 AD, presents a view of the very late 1 BC birth of Christ as being more than adequately corroborated.

THE ISSACHARIAN FACTOR

As an object lesson about the ever-relevant principle regarding matters of history related to the anticipation of prophesied events, and here, referring to how Christ's return can be viewed (i.e., his appearing to rapture his Church), consider the 2000th birthday of the Church in 2032 AD. Yes, passage of that date, without the 7-year tribulation occurring, is to verify that the to-be-discussed anciently proposed 7000-year timetable for the history of mankind—which posits precisely 2000 years for The Church Age—is not to be taken in the most strict sense of establishing cut-off dates. Regardless, the principle remains about the value of taking steps toward learning how one may glean such Issacharian "understanding of the times" in order to "endure to the end" with obedience about the Scriptural indicative for the Church to **not** be overtaken in surprise, as if by a thief (I Thessalonians 5:4).

The Church avoids this type of thief-like surprise by becoming familiar with, practicing, and internalizing such evaluative biblical exercises, thus assisting one in, as we have said, continuously and exegetically "circling a few dates" (as postulated earlier with regard to how early AD biblical students could have accurately identified the prophesied time for Christ's triumphal entry into Jerusalem). We shall, therefore, engage in this object lesson by providing an extended example of how

---

[92] See footnote 90 for this discussion point's source material.

[93] Read an excerpt from Andrew E. Steinmann's book *From Abraham to Paul: A Biblical Chronology* (St. Louis: Concordia, 2011), pp. 235-238 [footnotes removed]; see also his article, "When Did Herod the Great Reign?" *Novum Testamentum* 51 (2009), pp. 1-29.

one may use the availability of established knowledge to, in effect, benefit in this at least partially self-instructive sense. The ability to develop such sensitivity is biblically sound (as we are indeed biblically admonished to not be surprised, something that tentative "date circlers" would not be as prone to), so consider such thought processes as presented in the following study, starting with a question.

In consideration of our current perspective today, and thus to learn thereby, what qualifications have been established for that ancient-rooted case regarding 2032 AD, having been put forth early on as a possible terminus for Daniel's 70th week, thought to mark the end of our current, continuing dispensation known as The Church Age?

Of course, the historical segment of 2000 years, as this our template lesson posits, is placed within the additional 5000 years of mankind's entire history that spans the Bible's entire "week" of seven 1000-year days, as indicated in the scripture: "a thousand years in thy [God's] sight are but as yesterday when it is past, or as a watch in the night" (Psalm 90:4 / brackets added). Peter reiterates this concept: "with the Lord one day is as a thousand years, and a thousand years as one day" (3:8). Accordingly, further documentation (of the two-day/2000-year segment to serve its own part within the seven-day/7000-year span) has also been established, providing a double-reference view of Israel's seven feasts,[94] four of which have long been fulfilled by the time of this point of our well-penetrated stage into the 21st century.[95] Thus, beginning here, the above-mentioned instructive template that can provide an inspirational pattern for one to learn interfacing skills with biblical and historical data is offered.

To begin, consider that the seven feasts of Israel, besides having the face value associated with their yearly occurrences, may also function prophetically as rehearsals for past and future elements of Daniel's 70 weeks. In that sense of the feasts' divisions that have conventionally been appealed to

---

[94] For a more in-depth study of this topic than what this work offers, again, see Gavin Finley's online original-source material, at endtimepilgrim.com.

[95] The New Schaff-Herzog Encyclopedia of Religious Knowledge: "The early fathers most commonly looked for the second advent at the end of 6,000 years of the world's history" (Vol. VII, p.376). The Encyclopedia draws that conclusion from the writings of the early church, including Irenaeus, Hippolytus, Methodius, Commodianus, Lactantius, and Pseudo Barnabas. Significant Jews have also believed in a 7,000-year timeline (from four rabbis) recorded in the Talmud. The Book of Jubilees indirectly supports this by pointing out that Adam died only seventy years before his thousandth birthday, and tying that to God's proclamation that Adam would die on the same day that he ate the forbidden fruit (Jub. 4:29 / Genesis 2:17). Thus, Adam's death may be viewed as a double-reference; spiritually, he died instantly when he ate the forbidden fruit, and he died physically at the end of day one, just 70 years short of one millennial day. These terminal 70 years of the seminal head of humans bear a prophetic indication of the ominous "70 years have been determined" segment of multiple prophesies, a judgmental span of time that harkens back to this Adamic antecedent.

in order to identify the beginning and ending elements of The Church Age (which, itself, begins *after* the end of the first **4** 1000-year "days," thus established early on as totaling the passage of **6** 1000-year markers by the time of the end of The Church Age), we have, as alluded to, categorized the first four feasts as already being fulfilled in Jesus Christ's ministry. This leaves the final three feasts of our contemporary future that will be fulfilled in a manner that can be understood with this text's timeline interface of the final seven years of this 21st century under human government, which is the terminus marker that thereby also identifies the commencement of the millennial reign of Christ on the earth.

So then, in keeping with the instructive purpose of becoming more sensitive to biblical/historical insights in the Issacharian sense of "understanding the times," we will review the qualifications for Daniel's 70th week, terminating in that discussed year, 2032 AD, which, as also noted, would involve the correlation of: (1) the seven feasts of Israel (that always occur on the calendar dates that these biblical traditions have always been assigned[96]) with (2) the seven days of God's plan for mankind's history (before the new heaven and new earth realm ensues from then on, for evermore). Such a method of approach could be called the Issacharian factor.

First, let us examine the thinking that has been applied to the established case for the end-time relevance of the remaining three feasts of Israel, the idea that has been considered a part of a 2000-year panorama of history, spanning from Jesus being recognized as Messiah, the Prince (i.e., Palm Sunday of 32 AD), ostensibly extending to the end of the Church Age, which includes the last seven years thereof being Daniel's notorious 70th week, otherwise known as the seven-year tribulation period.

FEAST FULFILLMENT

In this double-reference view of the feasts as being historically panoramic, as we have established, four of the feasts have been fulfilled already. They are literally fulfilled in epic fashion right on those auspicious Hebrew calendar dates to which they have always belonged. As delineated below,

---

[96] In other words, to review and hopefully clarify, since all 7 feasts always occur in the same order every year, and since we are considering the yearly cycle's placements for the final 3 feasts of the 7-feast yearly cycle as being indicative of the tribulation's timeline of 7 years (thus also marking the commencement of the millennial reign beginning with the 7th feast, right after that same year's 6th feast), then the particular feast-dates that mark (1) *the* [5th feast] *beginning* and then (2) *the* [6th feast] *end* of the tribulation will each come from dates associated with different yearly cycles of the 7 feasts. Thus, the yearly cycle of the 5th feast, starting on some future Tishrei 1, will run along with its associated order of the 6 other yearly feasts' normal course for 6 years before that 6th year's Tishrei 10 **6**th feast signals the end of the 7-year tribulation (as illustrated on page 92).

this is true for each of what are known as the three spring feasts and for the fourth feast, which is the summer Feast of Pentecost. Regarding the first three feasts that will be discussed, they are indeed fulfilled in the priestly ministry of Jesus. He came the first time to his people as the ofttimes suffering servant, providing in himself an atoning sacrifice for Israel and all mankind as the prophesied sacrificial lamb. In that first coming, he also officiates as high priest in literally taking his own blood of atonement and placing it on the mercy seat in the heavenly temple (Hebrews 4:14-5:10). As shall be further established in the text to come, keep in mind that Palm Sunday occurs four days before the Thursday Passover (the first feast below), on which the crucifixion occurs.

1. Passover [status: **fulfilled**] Jesus (i.e., Yeshua) fulfills this
    feast at his crucifixion in the spring of 32 AD (i.e., on Nissan 14).

2. The Feast of Unleavened Bread [status: **fulfilled**] Jesus-Yeshua
    fulfills this feast at his burial in the tomb (i.e., just before sunset,
    marking the commencement of Nisan 15).

3. The Feast of First Fruits [status: **fulfilled**] Jesus-Yeshua fulfills
    this feast at his resurrection (on Nissan 17), during the spring "holy
    week" of 32 AD.

4. The Feast of Pentecost [status: **fulfilled**] God's Holy Spirit fulfills
    this feast on The Day of Pentecost in the summer of 32 AD (i.e.,
    exactly 50 days counted out from the latter Feast of First Fruits),
    marked by the outpouring of God's Holy Spirit.

The Day of Pentecost erupts into its New Covenant fulfillment on a grand and magnificent opening day, the very birthday of The Congregation (i.e., scriptural *Church*) of Jesus Christ. As the feast is being celebrated in that momentous year, the Holy Spirit is poured out upon the 120 in the famed "upper room." The Holy Spirit revival overflows into the streets of Jerusalem, then across Judea and out into the surrounding Gentile nations.

What a wonderfully double-referenced day this is! For the original Feast of Pentecost is celebrated at Mount Sinai when Moses brings the Law down from the mount, and thus the initial first century Feast of Pentecost is not only the prophetic fulfillment birthday of the born-again-of-the-spirit Church, it is also the birthday of Israel.

17

DANIEL'S CHURCH GAP

• •

THIS SECTION'S SPACE BEGINNING *HERE*, BELOW THE UPPER DOTTED LINE (AND FROM HERE, EXTENDING TO PAGE 102) marks off the intermediary span of time, the mentioned gap of 2000 years (i.e., a span characterized by a type of "sealed up" phenomenon from Daniel 9:24[97]), wherein the Light of Israel shines, evangelically (since 32 AD) going forth into the Gentile nations, mercifully dispelling the spiritual darkness (to continue through the range of our template teaching lesson about that traditionally posited cut-off for the end of the age, in 2032 AD, as we have seen). To rightly establish the teaching template's historical highlights, we must examine things (again, in some depth) from the beginning of The Adamic Age.

First, it is important to note that, unlike the way we measure days, months, and years, our weekly cycle of sevens has nothing to do with the science of astronomy—it is only known and used throughout all earthly cultures because of direct instruction from the one and only God (exclusively, of the Bible). There is no natural phenomenon that would influence ancient people to mark off days in groups of seven; virtually the whole world adheres to this practice because the whole human-ancestry font of Noah and his family adhere to it, having received it from Adam, who in turn received it from YHVH-God.[98]

In Genesis, we read what has been popularly referred to as "the creation week" of seven days, each of those days being very plainly distinguished with an evening and morning, demonstrating an ("Can

---

[97] Part of this "sealed up" phenomenon (mentioned first on page 75), aside from identifying the Church Age, refers to the span of time in which there is a partial blindness of Israel until the fulness of the Gentiles (to receive the Messiah) has occurred (paraphrased from Romans 11:25).

[98] Secular revisionists concoct contrary perspectives about the origin of the seven-day week. For instance, ancient Babylon is erroneously credited for the tradition, given that culture's assigned significance to seven celestial bodies (the Sun, moon, Mercury, Venus, Mars, Jupiter, and Saturn). Ancient cultures did indeed, of course, repurpose the seven-day Genesis 1 orally passed down tradition of the original (Adam's Eden) culture to suit their pagan worldviews.

you hear the words that are coming out of my mouth!") out-of-the-way, intentionally redundant, directly divine effort to inform readers that the days are each normal 24-hour periods. Authors and compilers did truly write the scriptures from their ancient point of view that did not conform to modern attempts to allegorize away the plain meaning.

The above-discussed 7 days of Genesis, being a double-reference key to the whole history of mankind, is a *reason* why God uses that particular amount of time to accomplish Genesis 1:3-31. Rephrased, the seven days is a Divinely intentional type of pattern for Adamic mankind's history that is thus decreed, foreordained by our Creator; therefore, God did not choose to renovate the planet instantaneously for the Adamic race even though he created the totality instantaneously in Genesis 1:1. Those who take this topic with *exegetical* respect thus don't have a problem with investigating the case for the 7000 years as a key to understanding God's eschatological plan principle, with the *strictest* cut-off dates in tow, or not.

Having addressed several elements that relate to the 2000-year epoch, or The Church Age epoch (a necessity that fits within the clarification about the double-reference of the Genesis work-week), one can realize that *the first 4000 years* (of the 7000-year plan of God for the Adamic race) refers to human history beginning from the time of Adam (and not from the beginning of the 1:1 universe), and then extending to the established date of when the Messiah Jesus Christ is "cut off," or crucified, in 32 AD. Thus, the subsequent 2000-year Church Age, including its last seven years, and then also adding the millennial reign which follows, brings us to the sum of 7000 years, as also accommodated in the continuing discussion of The Seven Feasts of Israel.

AFTER TWO DAYS, BY THE BOOK

On page 86, two sample scriptures are shared that indicate God's use of the 1000-year-day principle; following is yet another:

> "I will return again to my place, until they acknowledge their guilt
> and seek my face, and in their distress earnestly seek me." Come let
> us return to the Lord; for he has torn us, that he may heal us; he has
> struck us down, and he will bind us up. After two days he will
> revive us; on the third day he will raise us up, that we may live
> before him (Hosea 5:15-6:2, ESV, quotation marks added).

Exegetically, the above scripture's "After two days [of following the Messiah-rejecting tradition / brackets added]" phrase refers to "After the 2000-year Church Age," and then the "on the third day" phrase refers to the subsequent and final 1000 (millennial reign) years of the 7-day/7000-year total timeframe that encapsulates God's complete plan for Adamic mankind before the commencement of the eternal epoch of the new heavens and new earth realm.

According to the postulated study, that is, to our veritable activation of the "Issacharian factor," our instructional lesson thereby continues here in consideration of the decade that begins with 2020 AD, thus presenting a past consideration of prophetic context discussions, including the view that it would be the final full decade of The Church Age. As you may recall, the previous pages have explained the special double-reference prophetic role about how the first four feasts of Israel have indirectly delineated the passing of the first "four days" of the seven-day/7000-year period of history in the sense that the termination of those four feasts in 32 AD marks the end of the first 4000 years of human history, and thereby also marking the beginning of the 2000-year Church Age, amounting to 6000 years. Thus, as the Hosea citation above reviews this history by means of overlapping with the established Church Age, we then face the remaining double reference roles for the three end-time feasts that occur incrementally, each according to their own prophetic place in the context of the regular 7-feast yearly cycles. The recognition of these three remaining fall-feast roles as eminent 21st century events (thereby reiterating the fulfilment of the final 3000 years of that seven-day/7000-years total) thus composes The Church Age *through* the millennial reign. The illustration on the next page, then, is a preview of this study's to-be-further-discussed "Daniel's 70th week," the final seven years of the conventionally posited 2000-year Church Age, as well as the subsequent feast at the closing of the final seven years that mark the commencement of the Millennial Reign of Christ.

THE REMAINING THREE FEASTS OF ISRAEL DEPICTED AS THE END-OF-CHURCH-AGE FEASTS

(A couple Tishrei 1-10 range examples from the 2020 AD decade is on page 100.)

The "2520" figure (immediately below) and context are explained farther ahead in the main text.

$2520 \div 7 =$ 360 days (1st year) The (5th) Feast of Trumpets on Tishrei 1 (of a future year)

360 days (2nd year)—The 7-feast yearly cycle occurs

360 days (3rd year)—The 7-feast yearly cycle occurs

360 days (4th year)—The 7-feast yearly cycle occurs

360 days (5th year)—The 7-feast yearly cycle occurs

360 days (6th year)—The 7-feast yearly cycle occurs

360 days (7th year)—The 7-feast yearly cycle occurs, and results in:

—the end of anti-Christ's

blasphemous influence

—the end of the trampling of

Jerusalem

+ 30 days (added to the 1st through 7th-year feast cycles)

ends the 2550 days / composing the Tishrei 1 through Tishrei 10, 86-moon, 7-year, and 30-day period / During this final 30-day period:

—scales fall from Israel's eyes

—all Israel is saved (Daniel

12:11, Zacheriah 12:8-13:1)

—a final mercy-margin for

Gentiles also?

The (25-hour, 6th) Feast-Day of Atonement

spanning Tishrei 9-10

The Day of the Lord, the Second Coming of Jesus Christ

+ 5 days — five days for the judgment of surviving nations

of sheep and goats

The (7th) Feast of Tabernacles, on Tishrei 15, starts the 1000-year reign of Christ

But the next major prophetic event for our 21ˢᵗ century society that will occur at some point in proximity to the remaining three fall feasts, despite some infamous efforts of various false alarm date-setters, is the rapture of the church. Luke 17 discusses this "catching away" of the church occurrence when Christ comes, when he appears above (but not "landing" upon) the earth-scene that is in a business-as-usual worldly mode of sinful mankind, thus not during an apocalyptic setting, for they were buying and selling (i.e., not during an economic upheaval), planting and building, marrying, etc.[99]

WARNING-REMOVAL-JUDGMENT

Thus, according to the scriptures, Noah's and Lot's times provide parallels to the eminent rapture event, featuring: (1) *warnings* that are ignored or mocked, (2) eventual *removal* of the righteous (from the targeted place upon which God's wrath is directed, meaning including the tribulation period, thus upon the planet Earth and its inhabitants)…and then (3) the decisive act of *judgment*. In Noah's day, the ark is the step "(2)" *removal* before God's wrath falls; in Lot's Day, angelic escort is the step "(2)" *removal*; in 21ˢᵗ century time, the rapture is the step "(2)" *removal*. Regarding the removal of the righteous before any judgment is poured out, it is notable that the eight souls in Noah's ark are shut in safely seven days before the waters come; accordingly, there's no telling how much time *before* the 7-year tribulation the rapture occurs.

To continue "by the Book," though, the raptures (plural) will occur with "…every man in his own order" (I Corinthians 15:23), "order" being from the Hebrew word "tagmata," connoting a military camp or standard under which regiments are presented, as in a parade.[100] This refers to when Israel is gathered around the wilderness tabernacle in their orders when it is time to "move out," each in its own turn does so.

---

[99] Some "Bible students" complain that the word "rapture" isn't in the Bible; however, the phrase "caught up" is in the Bible, and "rapture" means "to be caught up." This is like the nonsensical complaint about the fact that the word, "trinity," for example, is not in the Bible, but is also exegetically well established. The Greek "harpazo," then the Latin "rapturo," led to the "caught up" usage, as in I Thessalonians 4:17.

[100] For an in-depth study, read Jack Langford's *The Three-fold Order of the Resurrection*.

18

WHAT'S TAGMATA?

TAGMATA, AS PREVIOUSLY INDICATED, IS THE ORDER OF THE END-TIME RAPTURES, A THREE-FOLD PHENOMENON, aptly correlating to the three end-of-year or "end-times" harvest feasts of Israel, as the "order / tagmata" of I Corinthians 15:23-24 below specifies, indicative of, and thus paralleling:

–   "**Christ** the first fruits" (verse 23b) _**ascended**_, caught up,
    "raptured," etc., harking back to the crop sheaf of barley
    being waved up to God as an early harvest sample during
    the Feast of Unleavened Bread;

–   "_**Christ's**_ [_possessive form plurality_, referring to the raptured
    living Church and earthly corpses thereof] **at his coming**"
    (verse 23c / brackets added) before the tribulation, harkening
    back to when the fulness of harvest comes;[101]

–   "**Then cometh the end**" (verse 24) of the tribulation when the
    earthly corpses of all Old Testament forward-looking saints are
    raptured into glorification with their heavenly spirit-body
    counterparts, such as, for example, when Job will be raptured;
    indeed, _when_ "he [Jesus] shall stand at the latter day upon the
    earth…[when] I [Job] shall see God" (Job 19: 25-26 / brackets
    added). This is the time of Matthew 24:29-30, when "[i]mmediately
    after the tribulation…then shall appear the sign of the Son of man
    [Jesus] in heaven…the Son of man coming in the clouds of heaven
    with power and great glory" (brackets added).

---

[101] This part of the whole rapture procession includes only _The Church Age's_ "dead in Christ" as well as those "which are alive and remain," all according to I Thessalonians 4:16-17.

Thus, regarding this latter "Then cometh the end" point, immediately after Job dies his natural Old Testament death, he enters paradise in the belly of the earth (Matthew 12:40) in the form of his own spirit-body (just as Moses and Elijah appear with Jesus in their own spirit-bodies, transported as they were from paradise to the mount of transfiguration / Matthew 17:3). Jesus descends into this paradise section of captivity (Ephesians 4:8-9) that is composed of all such Old Testament saints who yet await the glorification of their bodies, meaning, awaiting the unification *of their biological remnant corpses*, wherever their remains may be, with these their heavenly spirit-bodies.

Whether these Old Testament saints are transferred out of earth's belly "paradise" into the "third heaven [*beyond* earth location][102]" that Paul visited, with Paul still calling *it* 'paradise' / II Corinthians 12:2-4—a proposition that, if valid, could have occurred with the Jesus "leading captivity captive" incident, *or not*,[103] the fact is that such Old Testament saints will enjoy becoming raptured/glorified in their respective turn according to the I Corinthians 15:23-24 scriptures that are itemized above. Job and other Old Testament saints are "with God" in the form of their spirit-bodies ever since the time of their natural deaths. The idea is that, as Job is speaking in 19:25-26 in the context of his Old-Testament-time fleshly physique, the time he is prophetically referring to is thus the time when his fleshly physique will see God; otherwise, if he is referring to his paradise spirit body, Job sees God upon his own natural death, which, apparently then, is not what is being referred to. That referred-to time when the elements of Job's long-dead fleshly physique are glorified/united with his spirit self from heaven, and thus indeed when his fleshly physique (though modified) will see him, is indeed at the end of the tribulation period.

And with regard to the second part itemization, "Christ's [raptured church] at his coming," as with the times of Noah (i.e., when "they went...into the ark...the Lord shut him in" / Genesis 7: 15-16) and Lot (i.e., "the angels hastened Lot...Haste thee, escape thither; for I cannot do any thing till thou be come thither"/ Genesis 19: 15-16, 22), neither are the true spirit-reborn believers of The Church Age to be included in the earth setting where God's wrath takes place (I Thessalonians 5:9-10). The disciples may have thought that their several Matthew 24 questions to Jesus (i.e., "... when will these things be...what will be the sign of your coming [and of] the end of the age?"[104]) are synonymously the same question. Jesus' answers result in disagreeing discussions among today's Christians, raising the further question, "Why doesn't Jesus simply provide straightforward answers, as definite as some other biblically prophetic timetables?"

---

[102] brackets added

[103] The exegesis for this belief is not as nearly cut-and-dried as the popularity of the traditional belief itself.

[104] brackets added

SEALED UNTIL

For one thing, God no doubt wants every historical period to be full of anticipation for Christ's return. That is in keeping with a primary reason for this text's usage of the current teaching template about developing Issacharian sensitivity. Also, just as Satan is kept unaware of the consequences of "crucifying the Lord of Glory" (through Old Testament vagueness about the resurrection / I Corinthians 2:8), God keeps the future at least somewhat obscure to continue to confound them; after all, Satan knows the scriptures, and certainly even he isn't ignorant enough to disbelieve them (see James 2:19). But remember, it is also scripturally true that "this day [of 'a thief in the night']" will not overtake or surprise spirit-reborn believers (I Thessalonians 5:4). Jesus also tells his disciples that he has many things to say to them, but they couldn't bear them at that time, but when the Holy Spirit comes, he will guide us into all truth…and he will show us things to come (John 16: 12-13), further harkening back to the Daniel 12:4, 9 truths: "O Daniel, shut up the words, and seal the book, even to the time of the end…for the words are closed up and sealed till the time of the end." Apparently, as the end of "the last days" draws nearer, the release of more revelation about the end-times is sanctioned through the Spirit of God.

A conclusion exegetes may reach, then, includes the observation that, in Matthew 24, Jesus responds to the disciples' questions as separate rather than synonymous events, describing aspects of his as-yet future initial coming (to appear above the earth, prior to the 7-year tribulation, to rapture his church), as well as aspects of his Second Coming (at the end of the 7-year tribulation), necessitating a correlation with other scriptures in order to discern the differences between the two events, as the past few pages of this subject have explored. After the spirit-reborn Church of Jesus Christ is raptured (literally, "caught up"), to go and then participate in the benefits of heaven, the world's business-as-usual ruse will dovetail easily into the start of the tribulation period's "peace and safety" con (I Thessalonians 5:3-6). One of the initial acts of the anti-Christ will include "the covenant of Daniel 9:27," the official confirming of the 7-year peace treaty. This occurrence marks the beginning of the tribulation period (i.e., Daniel's 70th week).

In sharp contrast to the unknown time of the first harvest rapture of the church (i.e., the resultantly yielded "much fruit" from Christ's sample sheaf sacrifice of himself), seven years and thirty days later than the confirming of the anti-Christ's treaty, the Second Coming of Christ upon the earth—not just in the air this time—will occur as with the dependability of an immutable alarm clock. Any Bible student living during the tribulation, among others who miss the rapture (for studying the Bible, church attendance, being good, etc., is not the plan of redemption whereby one is transferred from the kingdom of darkness into the kingdom of God), can then start counting, knowing that seven years later, Daniel's 70th week (and then the thirty more days) will be over—disqualifying the rapture of the Church occurring "as a thief in the night" (I Thessalonians 5:2), for it would then be known exactly when he is coming if that is the case.

Or, conversely, the apostle Paul eased the early Church converts from their unnecessary concern that the Second Coming already occurred. He informed them that "the lawless one" (the easy-to-identify anti-Christ of Daniel's 70th week) would have to come first (II Thessalonians 2:1-9); and when the mid-tribulation's equally obvious "abomination of desolation" occurs (when the anti-Christ publicly declares himself to be God, and also officially breaks his peace pact with Israel), the anti-Christ will again thereby be unquestionably identified. Once that future event takes place, again, anyone can count 3.5 years to the end of the second half of the tribulation. Indeed, Jesus indicated that "immediately after the [7-year] tribulation" (Matthew 24:29 / brackets added) his coming will be "as the lightning cometh out of the east, and shineth even unto the west; so shall also the coming of the Son of man be" (Matthew 24:27).

The following discussion of the remaining three feasts provides a review and further elaboration of the events discussed and illustrated above. The format of the following discussion could be thought of as having a telescopic intent, revealing incremental truths of the prophetic subject as we advance, an intentional and hopefully helpful form of light review.

As established, the rapture of the Church, composed of biblically spirit-reborn believers, occurs at some point (known only to God) before the fifth feast, otherwise known as The Feast of Trumpets (recall the first four feasts from page 88):

5TH FEAST

The Feast of Trumpets (translated: "head of the year") is called Rosh Hashanah, or also, Yom Teruah [status: **unfulfilled**]. This feast always begins on Tishrei 1 of the Hebrew calendar. This epic future Rosh Hashanah will be a blockbuster day in world history. This awesome future Hebrew "Day of Blowing" will be the triggering event associated with Daniel's 70th week, ushering in the final seven years of this age. Daniel 9:27 refers to the infamous seven-year treaty covenant that will initiate The Feast of Trumpets. When we measure out the timeline between this fifth feast, The Feast of Trumpets, *and* the sixth feast event—The Day of Atonement—we have seven years, occurrences that bridge the *86* (and not 87) Tishrei-to-Tishrei moons, the timeline thus extending 2550 days inclusive. This is a precise match for the 1260 + 1290 = 2550 days, the timeline defining the final 7 years (plus 30 days) of this age, as also illustrated on page 92.

Of course, part of the history, pertinent to our instructional Issacharian factor template here, and as some readers may recall reading about in related world news releases, the Bible's mid-tribulation "wormwood" asteroid (of Revelation 8) is on record, the NASA-named asteroid *Apophis*, referring to its Earth flyby of Friday the 13th of April 2029. Indeed, such type of a trajectory as this will eventually be the one that God will use to fulfill the in-any-case inevitable prophecy.

And regarding the previously mentioned "plus 30 days" specification, John tells us in Revelation 13:6 that the woman of Revelation 12 is carried away on the wings of a great eagle to be nurtured in a wilderness place for a period of 1260 days. Eight verses later, in Revelation 12:14, the very same message is offered, but instead of "days," the description of "a time [i.e., 1], times [i.e., 2], and half a time [i.e., .5 or ½]" is used, or the sum of 3.5 years. Again, this also refers to 3.5 biblical or lunar years; 1260 ÷ 3.5 = 360. So, the two halves of the 70th week are each time-spans of 1260 days, adding up to 2520 days. In Daniel 12:11, we learn of a 1290-day figure that correlates to the time-span from the mid-portion of the tribulation (marked by the cessation of the temple sacrifices and the abomination of desolation / Daniel 9:27) to the end of the age (that is marked by the Second Coming). What is the significance of an "extra" thirty days provided in the context of Daniel's 70th week calculation? It is clear from Scripture that the reign of anti-Christ will end after the second span of 1260 days (Revelation 13:5), and the trampling of Jerusalem will also cease after those 1260 days, or 42 biblical months. After those two 1260-day halves of the 7-year tribulation have expired, Daniel's extension of thirty days may see transitional events, addressing the dealings God has determined for his covenant people (the Jews).[105]

---

[105] The transitional margin of time between the end of the anti-Christ's 7-year rule and the beginning of the Millennial Reign proper, whether it results in any further mercy-margin days (of the above Daniel 12:11-12 potential) for the Gentiles (or not) before the separation of the sheep from the goats upon Christ's return, *will* see all Israel saved.

19

"EXTRA, EXTRA," READ ALL ABOUT IT

THUS, THIS TIME PERIOD COULD POSSIBLY BE THE TIME THAT IS SPARKED BY THE EXTREMELY DESPERATE NATURE of worldly circumstances—and thus a time when spiritual scales fall as prophesied from the eyes of many, causing "all Israel … [to] be saved" (Romans 11:26; Daniel 12:11, and Zachariah 12:8-13:1 / brackets added), revealing a tremendous revival of those Jews who are alive at the end of the tribulation, finally being tilted enough to repent and accept their long-available Messiah. This may also be indicative of a mercy-margin for the surviving remnant of the spiritually lost Gentile world, the air having been cleared of the failed influences of the anti-Christ and the trampling of Jerusalem, etc., thus possibly yielding a chance for repentant inspiration before the judgment upon the nations (which occurs before The Millennial Reign proper begins). Indeed, the 144,000 Jewish converts, and angels, are a part of the Gospel-ministry during the tribulation (Revelation 14:6-10), and they are fit ministers of such a proposed post-tribulation margin for extended preaching, direction and mediation of any possible final offer of mercy from God if it is to be offered then.

On day 2550 (of the seven 360-day years, plus 30 days), The Day of Atonement will indeed occur, an apt thematic title in hindsight, suggestive of the proposed conversion activities that have been referred to. Considering our Hebrew calendar, then, running out to seven years, or 86 moons and 9 days from Tishrei 1 of various future time-range candidates, we discover that the discussed day 2550 brings us to a highly auspicious terminus date. Of course, we arrive precisely on the 10th day of Tishrei, that awesome Day of Atonement (i.e., see the "**6th feast**" proper, three pages ahead), also known as the Day of Reckoning, the Day of Accounting, the Day of Sentencing, the Day of Pardoning, the Day of Covering, and Yom Kippur. When the sun sets before this awesome future Yom Kippur, space-time will be unzipped to reveal the coming Messiah. This is the Apocalypse, the fulfillment of the Revelation of Jesus Christ, the great Day of the Lord.

This day of ultimate Return will unfold exactly as Jesus outlined in the parable of the tares. The tares will be gathered first (Matthew 13:30). God's wrath against sin will fall specifically and personally upon the heads of the wicked, those who harden their hearts against God's one and only spiritual-rebirth escape plan through scripturally expressed repentant faith in the shed blood

99

of Jesus Christ. Angels will swoop down upon the ever-duped ones and the wicked, who will then be plucked up, kicking, and screaming in well-founded terror. They will be carried off to their destruction in the form of eternal, conscious torment to personally pay the penalty for sin even though Jesus paid the price for them, if only they had been willing to receive. The righteous will see this (Psalms 91:8).

As the first four feasts of the seven-feast tradition divinely align with the event-dates of the holy week and Pentecost, so also, then, the final three feasts of that seven-feast tradition are expected to align with the event-dates associated with the beginning of the tribulation, and then also for the Second Coming seven years and thirty days later, which itself signals the commencement of The Millennial Reign. Thus, the seven-year and thirty days timespan implicating these final three feasts is expected to transpire in sync with the mentioned 86-moon phenomenon as illustrated (back on page 92).

ESTABLISHED SAMPLES OF TISHREI-TO-TISHREI

As the reader may recall from familiarity with related reports about this subject, and thus as a handy object lesson to apply in our instructive "Issacharian factor" template, consider the associated notoriously specific date ranges below that have become a part of this prophetic nomenclature. The material can be "instructive" in the sense that, at *whatever* future time the tribulation occurs, the subject 86-moon elements, as indeed offered for review below, will absolutely characterize that rightly-called "Daniel's 70th week." So thus, as the two forms of such 86-moon elements have been established in the 21st century's third decade matter-of-record, feel free to re-consider them, the 2550-day Tishrei-to-Tishrei periods of the celebrated 19-year, 235-moon Metonic cycles:[106]

(1) September 28, 2022 to September 20, 2029 and
(2) September 24, 2025 to September 16, 2032.

Remember these? The passing of any such date ranges without incident, meaning any such ranges beyond these established Issacharian factor examples, will always and inevitably point to some yet-future fall season on the first day of the Tishrei moon, eventually to mark the beginning of the tribulation period, the ultimate mind-blowing Feast of Trumpets to explode into world history. Ironically, then, trumpets of celebration and fanfare will announce the coming of a satanic

---

[106] The Metonic cycle is a period of 19 years in which there are 235 lunations, or synodic months, after which the moon's phases recur on the same days of the solar year, or year of the seasons.

"peacemaker," a self-proclaimed prince, on this Hebrew New Year, marking the beginning of the 7-year tribulation.

The situation of the Church Age extending beyond 2032 AD, in terms of our instructive Issacharian factor purpose, may well be regarded as an add-on mercy margin, something that the Lord is well-known for. There's also the discussion to consider about the Matthew 24:30 matter of "the coming of the Son of man," as it relates to Jesus saying, "when ye shall see all these things" (verse 33), where the "all these things" refers to the Matthew 24 list of details that will take place before the alluded-to return of Jesus. The fact that one of the details in the list is the telltale "abomination of desolation" (verse 15) is consistent with this topic's understanding that the mid-tribulation is, of course, during Daniel's 70th week, and thus after the Church has been raptured.

As a part of the instructive template that we are using in our Issacharian factor exercise, and thus for a theoretical lesson, mentally take yourself into the position of one who lives beyond 2025 AD (which would be the first year of the tribulation if the 7000-year cut-off for Adamic history is to be strictly held, indicative of a 2025-2032 AD tribulation). This scenario is intended as a framework for considering whether or not it is scripturally prudent to believe that the born-again Church is raptured before the proposed 2000-year Church Age runs its whole course (i.e., to 2032 AD).

As a further Issacharian factor inclusion, juxtapose the latter consideration with the discussion of the 7-year tribulation overlaying the final 7 years of The Church Age proper. In other words, even though the by-then already raptured church will not be present at the time of the tribulation's beginning, "the Church" composed of new converts who get saved during the tribulation from the preaching 144,000 as well as from preaching angels may merit such a titled inclusion with the body of Christ. With this understanding, The Church Age is understood as running its whole course by means of the tribulation saints.

Such internalized mental and spiritual interaction with scriptural understanding, whether this particular latter understanding was already known by particular readers or not, can in principle produce Issacharian factor progress in individuals. All that a "renewed mind" (Romans 12:2) is according to the Scriptures must be in play, though, lest one becomes lost in a carnally constructed quagmire, something that would not qualify as "redeeming the time" (Ephesians 5:16). If it all seems too much, though, continue to love Jesus and his word, growing in faith and love; with that, one cannot go wrong.

Having hopefully eased any possible sense of stress about this material, though, the instructional value about the topic remains compelling, as we then move on to further examining the case example of the 2000-year Church Age ending in 2032, truly, for Issacharian factor benefit. Thus, an established aspect of the associated timeframe's notoriety has been a form of appreciation for the equation "2032 - 7 = 2025," thought of as a latest time for the rapture's occurrence. Historically, this position has always been dependent upon the arguable validity of that early Church belief in a 7000-year timeline for the history of the Adamic race. One of the takeaways of this in-depth discussion is the distinction between date-*anticipation* and date-*setting*. The former could be included in those scriptural elements that inspire one to maintain ongoing readiness for the return of the Lord, always keeping up with our lamps (to be kept full of the oil of the Holy Spirit—enduring to the end, **whenever** that may be). Such is how one may—how the Church may—learn, including from its mistakes.

6TH FEAST

The Day of Atonement [status: **unfulfilled**]

The Jewish nation and "all Israel" will be saved; the trumpets of jubilee are also blown on this same day of atonement; this is The Day of the Lord, and Doomsday for the unrepentant wicked. This feast always ends on Tishrei 10 of the Hebrew calendar, the last day of The Times of the Gentiles, thus of this present evil age.

Immediately below is the dotted line, marking the timeline's end of Daniel's Church Age gap, the seven years of tribulation, having run its course, plus thirty days. (The beginning of Daniel's Church Age gap is marked with the initial dotted line on page 89.)

....

7TH FEAST

The Feast of Tabernacles [status: **unfulfilled**]

This feast fulfills the great return of Christ to the earth, initiating the Millennial Reign of the long-resurrected Messiah, returning in the flesh from heaven *with* his Church, who were raptured/glorified seven years earlier, now to rule the earth with Christ. This ending of the tribulation period is also the time when all Old Testament forward-looking saints, gathering in paradise/heaven since the time of Adam, are raptured/glorified, as alluded to (on page 94) regarding Job when "he [Jesus] shall stand at the latter day upon the earth…[indeed when] I [Job] shall see God" (Job 19: 25 26 / brackets added).

This event marks the beginning of the Millennial Reign of Christ on the earth "in Person." Jesus will rule the earth along with his army of administrative, and now glorified, saints who return with him from heaven, where they have been for the past seven years of the tribulation period. The millennium will begin with a righteous God; his glorified saints; his righteous elohim of old; and natural seed Adamic "sheep (not goats)" humans who got saved during the great tribulation, who were not executed by the anti-Christ government, and did not die by means of any of the other horrors of that time. Satan will be bound; the curse of Genesis 3 will be lifted; universal healing will occur for the natural seed humans; lifespans will revert to those of prediluvians (900-plus years, when a 100-year-old is still considered to be in his childhood / Isaiah 65:20); all animals will become completely tame; and would you believe "ETCETERA"!

Iron Rule

The "he [Jesus] will rule them with a rod of iron," or with stern authority, includes an understanding about some of the perhaps billions of children who will be born in the millennium (who will grow into adulthood), epitomized at the end of the millennium when, get this, after centuries of God-Jesus benefits on open display and experience for all, and then when "satan is loosed for a season," he, satan, will actually gain a human following again! (Talk about one "born every minute.")

The forces of God who meet them will not be defunded; this "human following" event personifies the foolishly glamorized "streak of rebel pride" that fallen Adamites have shamed themselves with since the Garden of Eden, now more accurately reconfiguring the delusion to be openly seen for what it has always been—the, in essence, "I did it my way" self-deception of failing to recognize the marionette way in which such spiritually lost individuals have been played by the only sometimes well-camouflaged suggestions of fallen elohim influences of the world. Their last hurrah protest that gathers and then surrounds the holy city at the end of the millennium will be suddenly destroyed by the fire of God, and they will be no more, that is, no more on earth.

20

JUST A MATTER OF TIME

THIS IS THE TIME OF THE GREAT WHITE THRONE JUDGMENT WHEN ALL SPIRITUALLY FALLEN PEOPLE, FROM THE TIME of Adam throughout history to the last person who died in the Millennial Reign, for even hell will give up its dead to mandatorily attend, stand before God the Father's throne. The dead in hell are as those who are held in jail without bond until this trial. As The Great White Throne Judgment is focused on those who never properly/biblically received God's offered plan of redemption through the rebirth-causing repentant faith in the atoning blood of Christ, all such attendees shall receive the same dark sentence to be "cast into the lake of fire…where they shall be tormented day and night eon after eon."

After The Great White Throne Judgment, God creates a new heaven, new earth, and new Jerusalem, a Jerusalem that will rest upon the new earth, not in heaven as in former times, a set-up that shall continue on forever and ever, a kingdom that will increase throughout the cosmos, never again to know any iota of evil at all. It is written.

*

If you, the reader, would like to be on "the good side" of the discussed inevitabilities of God's plan, you must repent, believe the gospel of Christ's shed blood that is given as full payment for your sins, and then properly receive him as such. How?

"…if you confess with your mouth the Lord Jesus, and shall believe in your heart that God raised him from the dead, you shall be saved. For with the heart man believes unto righteousness, and with the mouth confession is made unto salvation" (Romans 10:9-10).

Do not yield as if to do so with a degree of eye-rolling hesitancy, but in a manner of striking the ground a multitude of times with that fistful of arrows (a la II Kings 13:18-19). You could respond spontaneously to God's word, as the admonishment in the verse directly above indicates, or do so with the help of this suggested prayer to God:

> Dear God, I repent of my sins. I believe the gospel of
> the resurrected Jesus, and I receive him right now into
> my life as my Savior and also as the Lord of my life.
> Continue to complete this good work in me as I begin
> the lifelong process of renewing my mind through your
> word, the Bible. Amen.

If you indeed repented and received Jesus, you just made the wisest decision of your life, by far. One of the important next steps is to submit yourself to God's word in the sense of finding a local church home that believes in, preaches, and teaches the Bible. Hebrews 10:25 tells us— "us" referring to biblically born-again believers—to *not* forsake the assembling of ourselves together, but to attend so much the more as the day of Christ's return approaches.

The latter paragraph's emphasis upon "us," referring only to those who are born again, does not mean that those who are not born again should refrain from going to church, unless the church is one that falls short of overtly conveying the Bible's plan for redemption. These types of organizations function, perhaps unwittingly, to lull people into a false sense of security until they die with an unregenerated spirit and go to hell. These ineffective "ministries" might produce congregants, for example, who mistakenly think or assume that joining a church (or mere church attendance, or "always believing, or being good, for a whole life," etc.[107]), qualifies as the one-time, out-of and in-to (i.e., out of Adam and in to Christ / I Corinthians 15:22) conversion that is instant by means of a person's repenting and receiving Jesus.

However, this conscious spiritual rebirth incident is none of those less-than things, and neither is the rebirth some arcane theological technicality, nor is it merely some higher spiritual gear that's optional to shift into while one continues upon the road of salvation that has "always" and already been achieved. No, rather, *the rebirth is salvation itself,* not a veritable feather in the cap of someone who professes to already be saved. Indeed, this refers to the very fulfillment of God's whole blood-covenant-based plan of redemption whereby the fallen human Adamic condition is finally remedied. To partake in the rebirth necessitates the prior acknowledgement that the subject individual is utterly lost until after the rebirth occurs. All humans inherited spiritual death from Adam's fall: "For as in Adam all die, even so in Christ all shall be made alive" (I Corinthians 15:22). That is why nothing short of the completely literal spiritual rebirth itself can save the soul.

---

[107] Another false doctrine includes the notion that being water baptized (which should be done only *after* one is repentantly born again) qualifies one as a Christian.

If you, the reader, have any capacity at all to understand or accept this biblical truth now, and if you are in your right mind, you will (if you haven't already) immediately repent and receive Jesus as your Savior and as your Lord before reading any further.[108] The eternal torments of hell serve as a perpetual memorial of God's rightful wrath against sin. Swallow your pride (or whatever hindrance that applies). Do not be a part of hell.

Hell is a converse form of revelation about the truth that God is worthy of being worshipped. This worthiness is not merely true only because of God's sheer omnipotence. It is not as if God is the result of some epitomal form of evolution through which he impurely exerts a megalomaniac insistence on worship from the lower life-forms. This biblical worthiness is an entirely legitimate and transcendent "phenomenon" that cannot be defined in earthly terms; there is complete rest and righteous reveling for all legitimately converted realists in the Truth of it. Hell is a converse form of parallel to this topic of God's worthiness to be worshipped in the sense that worldly rebelliousness not only errs in blaming God for demanding worship, but also errs in the sense of shallowly believing that hell is the ultimate example of overkill.

Missing from the worldly rebelliousness ilk is an understanding of the infinite difference between God and *anything less* than God. This speaks of the need for *mercy* from God for our inferior nature as the infinite absolute of life's purpose. Thus, the truth is underscored that if we were to know truth as it really is—meaning, the way God "knows" and is Truth—then we would see how infinite torment in hell for those who reject God's plan of redemption his way is completely just and equitably right. This point includes how humans are so prone to the ways of their inevitable nature of ignorance about the exceeding wickedness of sin, which is "simply" the inherited-from-birth nature of fallen Adam, thus also making us hard drive sin-machines in practice, who think and evaluate the Bible accordingly (i.e., wrongfully). The quest to be good does not have the power to reverse the consequences of the fallen spiritual nature. Good people don't go to heaven unless they become recipients of God's above-delineated plan of redemption his way.

It might help to think of it like this: When a person does get reborn, their information is recorded in the Lamb's Book of Life (Revelation 13:8), including the person's name, the date of their birth, and then the date of their spiritual *re*birth. That is why God-Jesus commands the wonderful expression repeatedly through his word: "Truly, truly, I say unto thee, Except a man be born again, he cannot

---

[108] Receiving God's one and only plan of redemption is not the result of the receiver being manipulated in any way, as the enemy of human souls (i.e., Satan and his minions) would have people think. However, even if one was to be "manipulated" into a sincerely acquired escape from hell and inheritance of heaven, it would be eternally more sensible than clinging to one's own inferior, eternally costly position.

see the kingdom of God" (John 3:3); "That which is born of the flesh is flesh, and that which is born of the spirit is spirit" (John 3:6); "Do not marvel that I said unto thee, Ye must be born again" (John 3:7); "Blessed be the God and Father of our Lord Jesus Christ, who according to his great mercy has caused us to be born again to a living hope through the resurrection of Jesus Christ from the dead" (I Peter 1:3); "for you have been born again not of a seed which is perishable, but imperishable, that is, through the living and enduring word of God" (I Peter 1:23); "who were born, not of blood nor of the will of the flesh nor of the will of man, but [born] of God" (John 1:13 / brackets added), etc.

Religion alone has been notorious for dancing around in proximity to the rebirth without activating the potential for rebirth, and that is A-Okay with the satan persona, the very crafty, avowed enemy of human eternal souls. Jesus regularly upbraids religious leaders for following traditions, beliefs and practices that are not scripturally legitimate. The extremity of this emphasis is in keeping with the "there's no going back" nature of Judgment Day. It's not a complex matter. If you have been trusting in some non-biblical form of religious traditions, and are thus thinking something to the effect of "But if I do this (the Bible's being 'born again thing'), it will at least imply that my lifelong religious ideas did not save my soul already," then you're beginning to get the picture. Formerly, the satan persona was the epitomal *arch*angel, and now fallen, but one who shouldn't be underestimated; he is supremely wise in evil, having honed his craft for millennia, and quite effective at playing the splitting hairs game to his kingdom's advantage. If this doesn't apply to you because you have been spiritually born again already, then *praise God*; truly, thank you for cheering the born-again Church on while doing the same type of overtly literal evangelical work as you also have opportunity!

To clarify, even though one would not have to *remember* the date and time of the entirely conscious act of repenting and receiving Jesus incident (as, of course, the Bible story conversions also intimate), the individual should certainly be able to remember that the conscious act did indeed *happen* on a specific date at a particular time. The "act" being referred to is nothing except the conscious repenting and asking-receiving incident when one receives Jesus as Savior and as Lord. It does not refer to a feeling, a participation in a ceremony, an a priori or epiphany experience/feeling while witnessing a sunrise, etc., when less than what the scriptures declare occurs or occurred. Such a life-changing incident would be recalled and emphasized during the rest of the person's life. You would already be established as a Bible person who has been born again, and you would be using your testimony to spread the Gospel. We are renewed day by day only after the one-time incident of the born-again conversion takes place. There must be something there to renew day by day. It wouldn't do any ultimate good to renew a fallen Adamic spirit day by day even if that included a person's improvements in behavior and obeying a bunch of scriptures that are less than what the rebirth scriptures necessitate (such as kindness a la Proverbs 11:17; or even treating people in loving ways, but without being born again, for instance, etc.). Thus, salvation cannot be earned by such actions.

If you are a brand new "repent and receive Jesus" believer, or if you go to an ineffective "church," seek out a church that has a vitally evangelical and missionary emphasis in keeping with a healthy New Testament congregation. Until you locate such a church in your region, feel free to join the highly recommended online congregation of "live.reslife.org."

Also, tell somebody that you gave your life to Jesus; it starts you off on the right foot, spiritually speaking; truly, such candidness about your newfound faith in Christ puts you on the good side of Matthew 10:32-33, for "[w]hosoever therefore shall confess me [Jesus] before men, him will I confess also before my Father which is in heaven. But whosoever shall deny me before men, him will I also deny before my Father which is in heaven" (brackets added).

Still holding out? Not your thing? Is hell your thing? No; you were not born for that. For the love of God, please get saved now.

ENDNOTES

1 (from page 1, footnote 1) This note includes a religion-comparing Venn Diagram; it conveys an awareness of the inherent "politics/marketing" phenomenon that attends worldview preferences, an awareness that rightly qualifies a general refutation of the most popularized, delusional notion consistent with a classic example of the propaganda device known as the bandwagon approach: "Science is true no matter what you think or feel" (i.e., "So, since the metaphysical attachments to the definition of what passes for 'science' today, as determined by those who share the same philosophical feelings and thoughts, are true by virtue of the fact that we declare it to be so, hop on our bandwagon, and then you can be *as right as we are*"). First, carefully consider the Venn Diagram illustration on the next page.

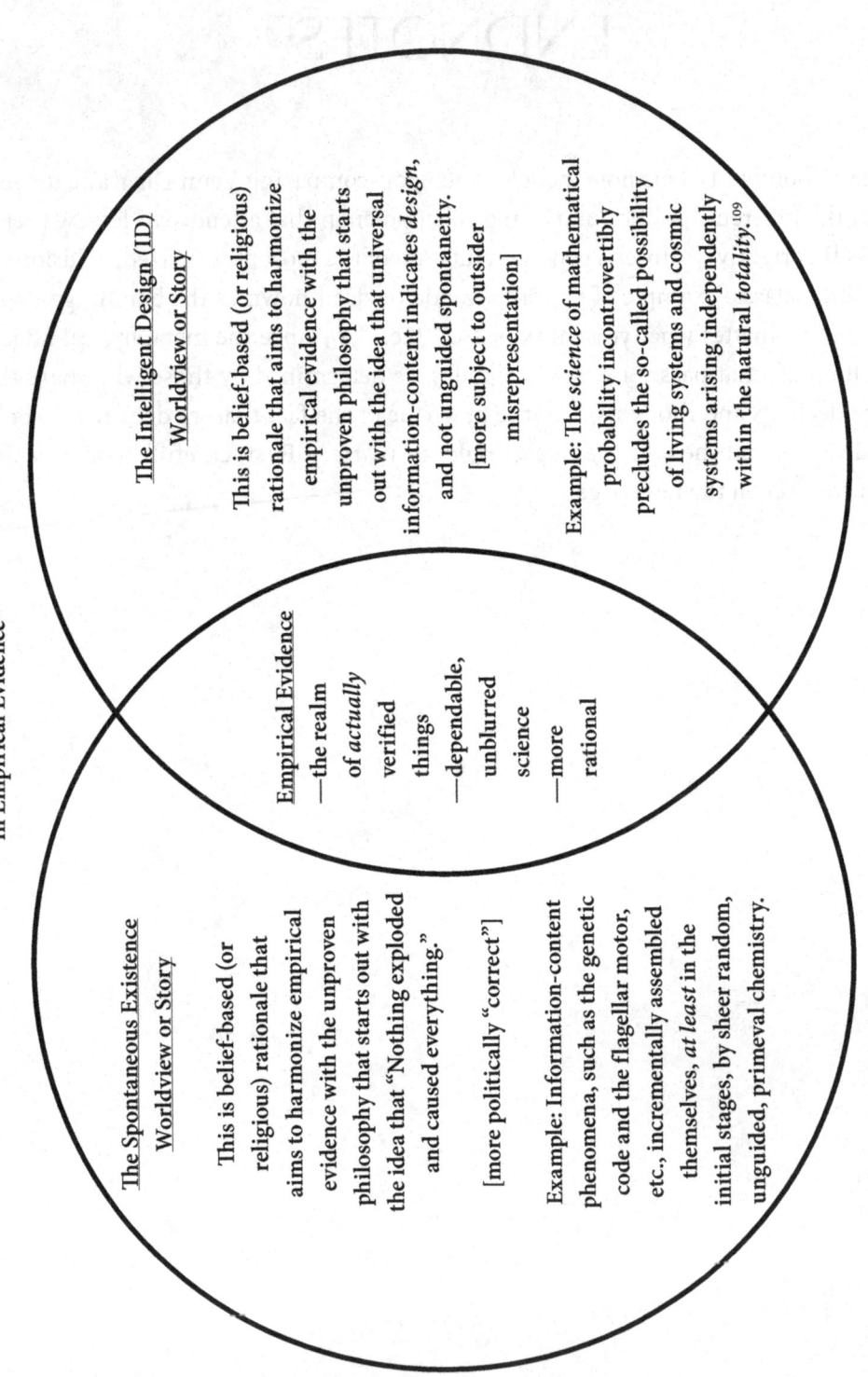

Two Worldviews that
Share a Great Interest
in Empirical Evidence

The Spontaneous Existence
Worldview or Story

This is belief-based (or religious) rationale that aims to harmonize empirical evidence with the unproven philosophy that starts out with the idea that "Nothing exploded and caused everything."

[more politically "correct"]

Example: Information-content phenomena, such as the genetic code and the flagellar motor, etc., incrementally assembled themselves, *at least* in the initial stages, by sheer random, unguided, primeval chemistry.

Empirical Evidence
—the realm of *actually* verified things
—dependable, unblurred science
—more rational

The Intelligent Design (ID) Worldview or Story

This is belief-based (or religious) rationale that aims to harmonize empirical evidence with the unproven philosophy that starts out with the idea that universal information-content indicates *design*, and not unguided spontaneity.

[more subject to outsider misrepresentation]

Example: The *science* of mathematical probability incontrovertibly precludes the so-called possibility of living systems and cosmic systems arising independently within the natural *totality*.[109]

[109] For an example of the science of mathematical probability, as opposed to metaphysical-philosophy-based speculation, being applied to the origin of life, see endnote 2 on page 113. / The Venn Diagram's overlapping area is not an indication of both worldview's equal alignment with the empirical content, but only that both worldviews draw upon the shared data to harmonize it with their favored model.

1 Timothy 6:20 warns against "oppositions of *science falsely so-called*" (italics added). Briefly, an example of this 6:20 sentiment's legitimacy is resident in the situation where, let's say, 95% of science textbook content can accurately be regarded as being empirically (and thus non-controversially[110]) verified, whereas 5% is governed by the consensus-assumption that the *non-empirically-verified worldview* of those who compiled the textbook is correct. Even though that 5% functions as the steering mechanism of the whole worldview system, that situation is not really the most unacceptable one, rationally speaking. The thing that is thoroughly unacceptable to proponents of. rationality is the false teaching (in schools, for example) that is inextricably tied into the erroneous viewpoint that 100% of the conventional textbook's so-incorporated worldview assumptions are in and belong in the touted category of "empirical science" as opposed to religious (i.e., belief-based) worldviews.

A case in point would now be in order. We have, for example, the empirically valid realities of natural selection, variation, mutation, etc. To coin an expression, this refers to the empirical category elements of *micro-evolution*. The gatekeepers of the notorious feelings-based metaphysical philosophy alluded to above have non-empirically extrapolated these elements into the popularized fiction of *macro-evolution*. To offer a template-principle of that "science falsely so-called," consider the wild speculation that "flying creatures have thereby transformed a la mutations-plus into all extant (and extinct) forms of flying creatures, nary a flying creature who did not have such an initial earthbound origin (including nonflying forms of insects, rodent-based forms, such as bats, for example, etc.)."

---

[110] "Non-controversially," meaning, for example, that Darwinists and Intelligent Design proponents acknowledge non-spun/pre-spun facts, such as: fossils exist, the earth's crust has strata, etc., ad infinitum. This understanding rightly does not include what might be called "less established worldviews," such as flat-earth proponents, "nothing exists" (i.e., "things don't exist") proponents, etc.

Such rhetorical art, composing funneled efforts of more directed energy to their favored mythology than to the genuinely empirical side of their "contributions," has the goal of blurring, or rather completely eradicating, the very real distinction between (1) their above-mentioned "feelings-based metaphysical philosophy" and (2) the empirically verified data that they endeavor to cajole into their blinder-clad worldview.

The oft-touted "great" Theodosius Dobzhansky is noted for the great pareidolian confession, "Nothing in biology makes sense except in the light of evolution," [111] that is, no such conclusive sense can be had (within the biological perspective) except for a fellow indoctrinate of Theo's favored *non*-empirically-verified worldview. Inherent to such a notion as Dobzhansky's is the idea that non-empirical belief-based (synonymously religious) views undergirding The Darwinian Mythology can be retained in "science," but non-empirical belief-based views undergirding Intelligent Design and its conclusively affirming science of mathematical probability (et al.) cannot be retained in science.

In other words, whatever one does, don't follow the evidence wherever it leads. However, you can and should claim to be following the evidence wherever it leads, as long as your leadings stay within the bounds of the philosophical assumptions of The Darwinian Mythology. Thus, to be a good indoctrinate, stay within your delusional lane. To speak from the promotional perspective of this widely popularized marketing type, "This is as it should be," for "we" are the "hierophants of an [otherwise] unapprehended inspiration"[112]; indeed, "we" are of the "We now know…[insert metaphysical belief element]" society, mystically akin to the ubiquitous "they" controllers of Men in Black fame.

To also *conclude* in this role-reversal vein, the less that "our" membership conveys any awareness about the above "(1) and (2)" distinctions (of three paragraphs ago), the more we are able to convey an impression to the little people that we are the rational ones in our strategically marketed "religion versus science" deceptive framing of the conflict. The rephrased goal of this conveyance is, of course, to forever evade the realization that our creed is, itself, just as non-empirically religious as those who hail from the opposite side of the Venn Diagram, whose worldview is—though unspeakably for us—at least as harmonious with the overlapped central area of empiricism as our own. Thus, by any means necessary, hide the truth that *everything* that distinguishes "evidence against ID" is non-exceptionally confined to the philosophical Darwinian Mythology's far left

---

[111] Pareidolia is a psychological phenomenon involving a stimulus wherein the mind perceives a familiar pattern of something where none actually exists.

[112] from Percy Bysshe Shelley's "A Defense of Poetry" (bracket added within the quotation)

side of the diagram. The challenge for our initiates is to thus reverse the impression of the latter sentence's truth by appearing to represent all manner of empirical data (albeit, inevitably, in non-scrutiny-passing ways) as being inherently bound to *our* view only, and, as much bound, then, to cast a sense of popular aspersions upon ID.

2 (from both page 11, footnote 22, and endnote 1's page 110, footnote 109) Consider an example of the science of mathematical probability being applied to the origin of life, using a citation from Marshall T. Savage's *The Millennium Project*: [113]

Our solar system is probably the only source of any kind of life in the universe. Those who believe that life must be a common phenomenon appeal to long, elaborate formulae to prove their case. They point out that there are hundreds of billions of stars in the Milky Way; of these, some 200 million are similar to the sun; around these other suns orbit 10 million earth-like worlds; life must have evolved on millions of these worlds; intelligent tool-users must then have developed hundreds of thousands of times; so there must be thousands of civilizations capable of star travel.

The argument is reasonable enough on its face, but the evolution of life is overwhelmingly improbable. The proposition that life ever evolved anywhere at all is to posit a miracle of Biblical proportions. If it wasn't for our manifest presence, the creation of life could be dismissed as a wild fantasy. Generating animate matter, at least in the fantasized initial stages, through random chemistry is so unlikely as to be indistinguishable from impossible. Yet here we are. Obviously, miracles do happen, but what is the likelihood of such a miraculous "accident"?

Let's presume that all that is required for the evolution of life is the formation of a single self-replicating chain of DNA. (A great deal more than just this chemical accident is of course required to produce single-celled organisms, and then a complete biosphere, and finally intelligent beings. But for the sake of argument, let's assume that a minimal chemical precondition is all that is required to set the chain of causality in motion that will eventually evolve you and me out of the mud.) As it turns out, the minimum chain length for self-replicating DNA is around 600 nucleotides. (Nucleotides are the building blocks of DNA, consisting of the base pairs of adenine-thymine or guanine-cytosine that form the rungs, and the phosphates which form the backbone of the ladder in the double helix.) Six hundred links is an exceedingly short DNA chain. Consider that a very simple virus contains 170,000 links, and a bacterium seven million; your own DNA chain is six billion links long.

---

[113] Little Brown & Co., 1994, pages 252-254 / ISBN-13: 978-0316771634

How likely is it that the primordial soup, given enough time, will cook up a strand of "Genesis DNA"? To calculate the odds of such an event occurring at random, we need to turn to "information-theory." This is an arcane branch of statistics developed to aid in the design of computers and telecommunications networks. Essentially, information-theory reduces the nebulous concept of "information" to exact mathematical quantities relating to message length and content. According to information-theory, a message with meaning can be interpreted as a level of probability. In other words: How likely is it that the message will be generated at random? This probability is dependent on the number of bits of information required to encode the message. The number of bits is then the exponent (base 2) of the number of random trials it would take to generate that message. In plain English, this means that generating even a relatively short message by random trial and error takes an enormous number of tries.

Words, like those you're reading now, contain meaning—at least that's the intent. In theory, the same message content could be generated randomly; using information-theory, we can find out what the odds are of a given message being generated by chance.

Let's use a very simple message: "See Spot run." This minimal message contains just thirteen elements: ten letters, two spaces, and a punctuation mark. Written English requires only about 50 symbols to convey any message: 26 letters, 10 figures, 13 punctuation marks, and blank spaces. The first position in our message has one chance in fifty of being an "S." The odds of generating a particular message one symbol long are 50 to 1. The second position has the same odds, so the chances of a message two symbols long turning up as "Se" are 50 x 50, or 50^2 to one. Every time a symbol is added to the sequence, the odds against that sequence go up by one multiple: three symbols—50 x 50 x 50, or 50^3 to one; four symbols—50^4 to one, etc. It is very easy to calculate the odds of any message being generated at random: The number of possible symbols is the base, and the base number is raised to an exponential power equal to the number of symbols in the message. The odds of generating "See Spot run." at random are 50^{13} to 1. To create this rudimentary message by accident would require 610,000,000,000,000,000,000,000 (six hundred billion trillion) trials. If a computer were programmed to generate a 13-character string at random, and created 10 million new strings every second, it would take the computer two billion years to come up with "See Spot run."

Information-theory shows why generating a 600 nucleotide chain through random chemistry is—to put it mildly—unlikely. The genetic alphabet is much shorter, containing only four symbols: A-G, G-A, C-T, T-C, but this doesn't help matters very much. The same rules of chance apply. The odds of generating a particular string of nucleotides 600 base pairs long are 4^{600}, or 10^{360} to one.

Did you get that? To generate a strand of "Genesis DNA" would take 10^{360} chemical reactions. That is a completely ridiculous number. Septillion octillion nonillion decillion doesn't even touch it. The only way to describe it is as ten nonillion nonillion googol googol googol. Surely, there must be numbers of equal magnitude available to rescue us from such overwhelming odds.

The oceans of the early Earth contained, at most, 10^{44} carbon atoms. This sets the upper limit on the possible number of nucleic acid molecules at 10^{43}. (This assumes that every atom of carbon in the ocean was locked up in a nucleic acid molecule—an unlikely state of affairs.) The oceans could therefore contain no more than about 10^{42} nucleotide chains, with an average length of ten base pairs. If all these nucleotides interacted with each other 100 times per second for ten billion years, they would undergo 3×10^{61} reactions. This would still leave them woefully short of the sample needed to generate a strand of Genesis DNA. To get a self-replicating strand of DNA out of the global ocean, even if it was thick with a broth of nucleotides, would take ten billion googol googol googol years.

But there are billions of stars in the galaxy and billions of galaxies in the universe. Over time, the right combination would come up somewhere—wouldn't it? Assume every star in every galaxy in the entire universe has an Earth-like planet in orbit around it; and assume every one of those planets is endowed with a global ocean thick with organic gumbo. This would give us 40,000 billion billion oceanic cauldrons in which to brew up the elixir of life. Now we're getting somewhere—aren't we? In such a universe, where the conditions for the creation of life are absolutely ideal, it will still take a hundred quadrillion nonillion nonillion googol googol years for the magic strand to appear. And that's before the rest of the elements of the mythology have to fall into place consistently, each element with its attendant comparable need to overcome such odds.

Assuming some radically different form of life, independent of DNA, doesn't really help. By definition, life forms will always be complex arrangements of matter and/or energy. This complexity has to arise out of chaos. Therefore, some initial degree of order must first just happen. Whatever the form of life is, its creation is dependent on the same sort of chance event that created our first strand of DNA. It doesn't matter what sort of coincidences are involved: the matching of base pairs, alignment of liquid crystals, or nesting of ammonia vortices; etc., whatever the form of proposed life, it will be subject to the same scientific laws of probability. Consequently, any form of highly complex, self-replicating material is just as unlikely to occur as our form. Simply put, living is an unlikely state of affairs.

When all of the fundamental constants underlying the bare existence of the universe are also taken into account, it becomes all too obvious for rational individuals that life is a sheer impossibility.

Bottom line: To understate, it is not more rational to believe in The Darwinian Mythology than to believe in Intelligent Design. / For more resources of this type, see endnote 19, page 161.

3 (from page 2, footnote 4) Why, amid all the creative/entertaining options, should the Bible be read literally? What is it about people's psyche, when considering the Bible, that influences them to negate this truth that it should be read with as much sense as when one reads the newspaper? Consider the following.

An important aspect of exegesis is to recognize literalism as the only legitimate way to understand the scriptures.[114] Language itself absolutely requires "literalism," an approach that acknowledges figurative or analogical expressions when the context demands the non-literal exception. If a literal interpretation is not used in studying the scriptures, there is no objective standard by which to understand the Bible, or anything else for that matter. Each person would be able to interpret anything and everything as he sees fit, which is the definition of the inferior "method" of eisegesis.

To offer a nonbiblical and hyperbolic example of the eisegesis principle in action, consider this claim: "Shakespeare's *Romeo and Juliet* is actually a presentation of an elaborate prophetic code that foreshadows the victor of the 2020 presidential election." "Genius" experts at rhetoric could have an interesting time drafting a defense for that ridiculous claim. Get the idea? In other words, with eisegesis, biblical interpretation devolves into "what this passage means to me" (or, to put it in woke squad lingo: "this is 'my truth' about this passage") instead of "the Bible says." Sadly, this is already the case in much of what is superficially called "Bible study" today, but, for example, every prophecy about Jesus Christ in the Old Testament was fulfilled literally; Jesus' birth, ministry, death, and resurrection all occurred exactly as the Old Testament predicted. Since Christians are commanded by God to "rightly divide the [biblical] word of truth" (brackets added), it must be recognized that scriptures can also be "wrongly divided," typically upon the no-holds-barred path of eisegesis.

For another example, it would make no more sense to use a figurative allowance about the way one should read a newspaper account (for instance, regarding the timeframe in which the events associated with a burglary occurred), than it would to use a figurative allowance for the way one should read a biblical account (for instance, about the contextual "evening and morning" timeframe sum of "days" in which the events associated with the Genesis 1 account occurred). "Regarding that

---

[114] For the sake of the accessible proximity of this endnote's context, it would be helpful here also to review the elements of eisegesis (i.e., the opposite of exegesis), referring to a subjective interpretation of scripture that expresses the interpreter's own ideas, bias, or the like, rather than the exegetic (objective) meaning of the text that is achieved by proper "interpretation" of the scripture considering all other also-rightly-divided scriptures that address the related subject. For an in-depth study of this, see: https://www.gotquestions.org/ dispensationalism.html.

newspaper article, dear, what do you suppose that the gun they said the burglar had symbolizes?" Uh, no.[115]

Thus, in view of the multitudes of explanations about various sides of the main (or any) debate, one must defer to the simplest and most direct view of the biblical revelation. Literary geniuses from any side of the debate can put forth seemingly difficult-to-dismiss *rationales*, but in the final analysis, one's distillation of the biblical story must favor the necessity of holistic harmonization and literal simplicity—that is, if that is what the individual is actually interested in. Even though such legitimate exegetes utilize word study data, they do not believe that sophisticated theological Capone-defense-attorney-type rationales (or downright eisegesis displays) trump the meaning of a simple "stop" sign to mean "go," not even when or if "the original Greek" principle is fancifully being appealed to.

4 (from page 2, footnote 5) Indeed, one calling upon "the Spirit's aid" presupposes that one has already properly repented and received God's established plan of redemption, and is no less, then, making one's way along the processional path of mind-renewal (i.e., "...be not conformed to this world: but be ye transformed by the renewing of your mind, that ye may prove what is that good, and acceptable, and perfect, will of God" / Romans 12:2). Becoming a biblical Christian, which is the only "kind of Christian" that ends up in heaven, is characterized by an incident/*moment* in time when one is "delivered...from the power of darkness, and hath translated us into the kingdom of his dear Son" (Colossians 1:13, et al.), a "phenomenon" that is not gradual. Thus, one becoming a proper recipient of God's only plan of redemption is not a process, but indeed is a one-time event in a person's life when one repents and receives Jesus. This does not refer to a "but I've always believed" mental assent or superficial acknowledgement, even if paired with a lifelong dedication to one's religious tradition(s).

The only thing that can reverse the consequences of the fallen spiritual nature that all humans inherited from Adam, the seminal head and thus also the spiritual head of the race, is to become spiritually reborn in that referred-to life-changing moment, such as the repentant thief illustrates on the cross, moments before he dies, thus a recipient of the "you shall be with me in paradise" destiny. It is not necessary to retain knowledge of the date and time of day wherein one thus receives Christ Jesus, but everyone who does so at least recalls that special incident when the reception was

---

[115] So, eisegesis is a form of the interpreter's personal "self-analysis" being displayed (i.e., an "analysis" of one's own psyche, **minus** any self-awareness of the interpreter that could otherwise cause the interpreter to realize that this is what's going on), rather than a legitimate reflection of the scriptures themselves.

so-consummated on a particular day, at a particular time, when one engages properly in the most overtly conscious action that one could ever do.

As previously noted, religious tradition indeed dances around the rebirth without ever attaining it; the "I've always believed" commonality makes one tie-game with devils, for "Thou believest that there is one God; thou doest well: the devils also believe, and tremble" (James 2:19). They, the devils, are thus at the "tremble at his word" (Isaiah 66:5) stage of belief, likely exceeding the degree of belief of those "always believing" humans who nevertheless have not decided to become born again according to the scriptures, even though they have been informed of the necessity.

One must step out of the seemingly impressive demon-level "believe and tremble!" mode into the legitimate BORN OF GOD mode (of John 1:13: "Which were born, not of blood, nor of the will of the flesh, nor of the will of man, but of God," or also of John 3:7: "marvel not that I [Jesus] said unto thee, Ye must be born again," etc. / brackets added). So properly becoming literally and spiritually born again is the farthest thing from a subconscious occurrence, and likewise, neither can the rebirth be whammied upon someone, for instance, upon an infant through baptism, which makes for a good anti-template illustration for understanding the danger of "the traditions and doctrines of man" negativity that Jesus despised so much (Mark 7:8). Baptism is absolutely meaningless unless the recipient has already been properly born again of the spirit according to the scriptures, for baptism is an outward, public sign/declaration of what has already occurred on the inside of the fully aware subject, prior to the baptism incident.[116]

A common defense-response from "traditions and doctrines of man" individuals, when such individuals become aware of the above biblical truth, is to pick out some former experience, a special moment or so-called epiphany, and then resolve to assign that past phenomenon in their thinking as qualifying them to be among those who have already become born again. With this "strategy," one can deceive oneself into never becoming a biblically born-again Christian. Becoming progressively more dedicated to one's traditional religious beliefs that are passionately believed-in is not being born again according to the scriptures. The main enemy that succeeds against everybody who needs to be born again, but does not become born again, is pride, the tendency to not want to step out because of what people fear regarding reactions from others if the faithful deed is done.

---

[116] Baptism's two elements that emerge from biblical "buried" and "risen" usages, are signified in the recipient's submersion into a body of water, and then being raised back up out of the water, symbolizing the literal spiritual resurrection from the dead by such a one **who already—previously—became a recipient of God's plan of redemption.** Thus, **after** such salvation, the person must be water baptized: "Buried with him in baptism, wherein ['wherein,' meaning 'and thus by the means of such baptism…'] ye are risen with him through the faith of the operation of God, who hath raised him from the dead" (Colossians 2:12 / bracket added).

After one biblically, repentantly, and prayerfully goes to Father God Himself, and makes it official—asking/receiving Jesus into one's life, as Savior and as Lord, one is indeed a *non-process* (sudden) recipient of being born again of the Spirit of God in that moment, *now,* a veritable "temple of the Holy Spirit" (I Corinthians 6:19), which, again, is an "out of" and "in to" experience. One is then obligated, again scripturally, to begin *the never-ending process* of mind-renewal, zealously and systematically engaged in the honor of replacing one's own worldly ways with exegetically legitimate biblical truth, not a self-righteous undertaking at all, but a requirement of God for those who know better than anyone that everybody who becomes born again and thus becomes bound for heaven is so-designated "as saved" only because of the boundless grace of almighty God. And doing the latter "process thing" without having done the former "*non-process* thing" (i.e., actually becoming born again!) does not save the soul. Selah.

For guidance about how to repent and receive Jesus, visit page 104 in the main text.

5 (from page 2, footnote 6) This is the companion proof, in lieu of Daniel's 70 weeks prophecy that shall come in its own chronological time in this work's main text.

DANIEL'S GREAT IMAGE

In Daniel 2, the ancient king of Babylon is mentioned, Nebuchadnezzar II. There is no longer, and really never was, any reason for intellectually honest individuals to entertain the notion that king Nebuchadnezzar is part of some ancient mythology. Archaeological verification to the contrary abounds, including "Nebuchadnezzar's cylinder" (in the British Museum), a record of king Nebuchadnezzar's collaboration regarding some contemporary building projects (i.e., temple restoration, ziggurat construction, etc.), including the interesting factoid that king Nebuchadnezzar's father's (i.e., king Nebuchadnezzar I's) palace also had to be repaired, as it was damaged by flooding. There's the Babylonian Chronicle clay tablet, describing events from 605-594 BC, including Nebuchadnezzar's invasion of Egypt, Judah's refraining of paying taxes/tribute to Babylon, and Babylonian sieges upon Jerusalem, resulting in the carrying off, for example, of Jehoiachin of Judah, among others (including Daniel in the 605 BC first Babylonian incursion). There's "Nebuchadnezzar's Brick," which includes an inscription noting the completion of a palace for Nebuchadnezzar in Babylon, written in the Akkadian dialect in cuneiform script. Many other such verifications have been discovered; as for the multitudes of cuneiform tablets that testify of the reality of Nebuchadnezzar, see such sites as https://www.reuters.com > us-israel-archaeology-babylon.

Of course, then, king Nebuchadnezzar is a real person, king of a real kingdom. The prophet Daniel, being among those who were taken to Babylon, is part of that sixth century BC reality. In Daniel 2:1-9, king Nebuchadnezzar has a dream that he becomes fixated upon to the point that he demands an interpretation of it (and issues a death threat against failure) without telling his proposed wise men, interpreters-to-be, what the dream was about, which these summoned "wise men" understandably admit they cannot do.

So Daniel prays to God (in Daniel 2:19-23), and God reveals that Nebuchadnezzar's dream had to do with the "latter days." The dream depicts a great image of a man who has a head of gold, chest and arms of silver, a belly and thighs of brass, two legs of iron and feet of clay and iron. Then a stone is hurled at this great image, striking it on its feet, blowing the whole thing to smithereens, to the point of powdering it, and then the stone fills the earth (2:34-35).

Daniel informs Nebuchadnezzar that the head of gold stands for the king's present kingdom of Babylon (circa 602-527 BC). Nebuchadnezzar is further informed that the Medo-Persians would overcome his Babylon (lasting from circa 527-336 BC). The Grecian Empire of Alexander the Great would be next (from circa 336-28 BC). Then, the Roman Empire would dominate (from circa 28

BC to 476 AD). In other words, the image was a timeline depicting Nebuchadnezzar's Babylonian Empire through succeeding world empires, the final empire (Roman) composed of some strong (iron) and some weak (clay) national components.

Of course, revisionist historian proselytes of the politically correct Secular Humanism cult, evading the implications of Daniel's 6th century prophecy (that disproves the humanist's spin on reality), insist that Daniel's prophecy is written after the fact. Overwhelming evidence, however, indicates that Daniel's prophecy is truly contemporary with the biblical times assigned:

- Parts of Daniel are written in an older Chaldean script that is consistent with 6th century usage, as exists in king Nebuchadnezzar's day;[117]

- The Dead Sea scroll's inclusion of the book of Daniel dates to 200 BC—of course, before the Roman Empire existed—and, notably, the scrolls are confirmed as being later copies of yet more ancient manuscripts, all written according to the beyond-strict scribal rules of Judaism;[118]

- There are many secular references to the book of Daniel dating back to around 300 BC;[119] and

- Royal names and other characters in the book of Daniel have been corroborated by archaeological discoveries (see sources in footnotes 117 and 118 below).

Two important elements of the above-expounded-upon image include the facts that whatever the "stone" part is, it destroys the image, and the stone then becomes beyond-mountainous in that it fills the earth. This mountain-plus, this "stone," is indicated again in Daniel 2:44, "And in the days of these kings [prophetically referring to the kings of the image] shall the God of heaven set up a

---

[117] Daniel uses the word "Chaldean" in reference to "wise men" (as in 2:2, 4-5, 10; 4:7; 5:7, 11). The book of Daniel describes the people of Chaldea (i.e., the "Kasdi" astrologers) with a phonetic shift that makes sense for a 6th century BC author living in Babylon, but which would clearly be a mistake for a 2nd century author in Palestine, as the revisionists contend (Robert Dick Wilson, 1917, Studies in the Book of Daniel, Grand Rapids, MI: Baker, 1972 reprint, 1:338-339).

[118] "We are able to compare for the first time in history the Hebrew and Aramaic of the book of Daniel with manuscripts of the same book that are about 1,000 years older" (Mertens, A. 1971, Das Buch Daniel im Lichte der Texte vom Toten Meer, Stuttgarter Biblische Monographien 12, Wurzburg: Echter Verlag. 1979:31).

[119] A five-sided clay prism found in Babylon includes the equivalent to the Aramaic name "Abednego," Daniel's friend; another name thereon is "Meshallim-Marduk," Nebuchadnezzar's official, named after a Babylonian god; etc. (from Istanbul Museum Prism #7834 found in Babylon, mentioning the court of Nebuchadnezzar; other above-associated references from column 4 of the prism).

kingdom, which shall never be destroyed: and the kingdom shall not be left to other people, but it shall break in pieces and consume all these kingdoms, and it shall stand forever" (brackets added). This is referring not only to the Millennial Reign of Christ, but ultimately, to the new heaven, new earth, and new Jerusalem kingdom that will never end.

As suggested, more specific and empirically verifiable prophetic evidence continues in the main text.

6 (from page 12, footnote 25) Regarding the Septuagint and the conventional Hebrew Masoretic text, the former is the ancient Greek translation of the Old Testament and quoted most often by the New Testament authors, thus quoted more by them than even the latter traditional Hebrew version. Most often, the Dead Sea Scrolls align more with the Septuagint, which is a plus, but even so, there is no translation that is better than all others for all Scripture verses. Dead-Sea-Scroll-inclusive texts, which is a more modern translation perk, offer greater validity to one's reading, such as the New English Translation (NET) avails, because such translations include text-critical elaboration about *why* its differing (better vetted) translations are used in light of such more ancient or more justifiable foundational texts. Thus, regarding how a choice between the Septuagint and the Masoretic texts should be guided, and considering that scribal variations characterize both texts, the rule is, whichever verse under consideration, from either translation, bears the best historical and exegetic reasons for how it gave rise to the other(s), is the best choice between the two (or more). Relatedly, Jesus and the apostles, including Paul, made no issue about the multiple *non*-identical Hebrew texts of the Old Testament, or about the non-identical circulating Greek translations, in the synagogues of their day. None of these texts doctrinally overturn what we think of as "the Bible" today.

7 (from page 13, footnote 27) The doctrine of the Trinity. Let's begin with a related truth; due to the fact that humans in the pre-glorified condition have far-inferior finite minds compared to the infinitudes of biblical revelation itself, we cannot yet mentally grasp such things as the truth that, for example, "rebels being consigned to conscious torment forever is not overkill" (for we are incapable of comprehending how exceedingly wicked and utterly alien the inherited fallen Adamic nature is), or such an incomprehensible truth as "the Father is God, that Jesus is God, the Holy Spirit is God, and there is only one God." Further, the word "Trinity," as true for the word "rapture," to use another example among so many other translated expressions, is certainly not found in all Bible translations. However, "rapture" means "to be caught up," which *is* in many English translations of the Bible; in like manner, the doctrine of the Trinity is absolutely true and legitimately biblical. Since such validity is well-documented and so broadly available, this work shall simply offer a source for any interested reader's verification: "gotquestions.org/Trinity-Bible.html."

8 (from page 14, footnote 30) The Darwinian Mythology principle, and therefore all of its so-principled offshoots, thus including the notion of cosmic evolution, displays a desperate strategy to reverse the impossible numbers that the science of mathematical probability inflicts upon the feelings of atheists (as endnote 2 addresses). Basically, their thinking goes like this: Given "the (mathematical, and thus literal) impossibility of life" evolving anywhere in the universe, "we" must concoct a way to reverse, to "turn it around," regarding only one universe in which to brew up the elixir of life's chain of causality. Therein, we have the metaphysical proposition that some form of a Big Bang did not bring into being merely *one* universe, but an *infinite* number of universes. A "truly" infinite number of universes can overcome any hard science odds that the more empirically consistent worldview of Intelligent Design can throw out there. "Voila!" as in "prest-o change-o," thus availing an adequate example of the "great" (satanic) marketing strategy that causes most people to fall for the framing of the controversy as being "religion (i.e., Intelligent Design) *versus* science (as defined by baseless atheistic metaphysical feelings)." Mercy, do "come out from among them," won't you?

9 (from page 20, footnote 36) Regarding "the mountain of God," Dr. Michael Heiser notes, "Zechariah 8:3 (ESV) echoes the same notion: 'Thus says the Lord: I have returned to Zion and will dwell [literally, "will tabernacle"; *shakan*] in the midst of Jerusalem, and Jerusalem shall be called the faithful city, and the mountain of the Lord of hosts, the holy mountain.' As anyone who has been to Jerusalem knows, Mount Zion isn't much of a mountain…This description would be a familiar one to Israel's neighbors, particularly at Ugarit. It's actually taken out of their literature. The 'heights of the north' (Ugaritic: 'the heights of *tsaphon*') is the place where Baal lived and, supposedly, ran the cosmos at the behest of the high god El and the divine council. The psalmist is stealing glory from Baal, restoring it to the One to whom it rightfully belongs—Yahweh. It's a theological and literary slap in the face, another polemic" (from *Unseen Realm*, Lexham Press, 2015, from page 227). Beyond this, the Revelation 21 "like-mountain" of God context presents the new Jerusalem's ultimate fulfillment of "the mountain of God" literality. None of this refers to any environment accessible to the king of Tyrus (or to the king of Babylon, etc.).

10 (from page 22, footnote 37) Information about the misnomer of "Lucifer" as a proper name:

There is some misunderstanding associated with the "Lucifer" translation (used, for example, in Isaiah 14:12). The KJV translators did not actually translate the original Hebrew word as "Lucifer"; they just used the same word that was used in the Latin Vulgate for verse 12, which reads as follows: "quomodo cecidisti de caelo lucifer qui mane oriebaris corruisti in terram qui vulnerabas gentes."[120]

---

[120] Indeed, one of the things that people (not familiar with original languages) don't commonly know is that they are encountering "Vulgatism" every time they read of Lucifer as a proper name for the sinless phase of the elohim

The underlined word there, "lucifer," is not a proper name, but is the Latin word for "morning star" (or sometimes "constellation"), from the words *lux* (light or fire) and *ferre* (to bear or to bring), meaning the bearer of light or bringer of fire, and then further referring to the illumination or brightness of the morning dawn. Lucifer is also one of the Latin names for the morning "star," Venus, as is the Greek word *Eosphorus*.

Now, as far as Hebrew is concerned, the KJV translation "O Lucifer, son of the morning" is from the text "heilel ben-shachar," *heilel* referring to the planet Venus and ben-shachar meaning "the brilliant one, son of (i.e., ben-) the morning." Ultimately, then, the Hebrew phrase in Isaiah 14:12 was translated by Jerome from the biblical manuscripts to be used in his Latin Vulgate because he believed the shining born of the dawn in Isaiah spoke of the morning star Venus, so he replaced the Hebrew and Greek meaning with the Latin name of the planet.

Another element of the "lucifer" usage story is seen in Job 38:32, where the KJV renders the Hebrew word as "Mazzaroth." It is reasonably assumed that the KJV translators did not know what the Hebrew word meant and could not translate it, so they simply matched up the Hebrew characters with their English character counterparts as best they could. Jerome, however, operated on a policy of trying to genuinely translate the original Hebrew, yielding "lucifer," or, rather, "morning star," an awfully close meaning to the original Hebrew expression.

For another example of the usage, in II Peter 1:19, the KJV renders the Greek word φωσφόρος (*phosphoros*) as "day star," where the Latin Vulgate has "lucifer." Again, the KJV simply reproduced the Latin from Isaiah 14:12, also apparently because they were not sure what the Hebrew rendering meant; the KJV translators knew Latin better than they knew Greek or Hebrew. So in the places where they were not sure what the Greek or Hebrew meant, they simply reproduced the Latin text. This has happened multitudes of times in the Bible. As a result, "Lucifer" has made its way into English Bible interpretations as another "proper name" for the devil but referring to him only before he fell.

Given an understanding of this information, it is not thoroughly unacceptable to use "Lucifer" as a handy colloquial reference to the character who likewise became popularly known as the

archangel who, as tradition has it, became the devil, and, consequently, sometimes object when they do or do not see such terminology and meaning applied to verses about Christ. For example, the Greek translation of II Peter 1:19 calls Jesus "Phosphoros," translated as "lucifer" (in Latin). Some translators have cloaked this issue so-to-speak by way of using the words "day star" instead. There is no blasphemy here, only a linguistic phenomenon. Considering popular (and likely harmless enough) impressions, thus for convenience's sake, at times, this work uses such "Vulgatism," retaining "Lucifer" for his pre-fall proper name.

archenemy "Satan" before he fell, even though the term is likewise not really a proper name, but a category of elohim beings. But here's the real point, regardless of whether "Lucifer," "day star," "morning star," or even "Jim Bob" or "Ralph" is used in Isaiah 14, an examination of the context is enough for any intellectually fair-minded person (who does not have a preconceived narrative to justify, or a plain truth to deny) to recognize a supernatural being, the "devil," as the elohim subject, and then also necessarily to reveal the time, circumstances, and accompanying humanoid contemporaries who witness the elohim being's fall, just as the Bible simply reveals. Forget "What do you think, dear, about what the 'people' and 'nations' symbolize in Ezekiel 28:19 and Isaiah 14:12?" If "dear" felt inclined to answer, though, the person could point out that "people" in Ezekiel 28:19, for example, comes from the Hebrew word bā·'am·mîm, a masculine noun, meaning "people," "folk," "men," etc.

11 (from page 25, footnote 43)

<u>The Five Pre-Genesis-1:2 Dispensations</u>

Dispensation One: Innocence

Satan in Council by John Martin

Figure 1, depicting Lucifer on his Isaiah 14:13 throne, indicative here in this study of his sinless existence that spans from his creation that took place sometime before the Genesis 1:1 event, to before his transformation into an evil being that occurs sometime well before the Genesis 1:2 event.[121]

---

[121] This image, "Satan in Council," is by John Martin, from *The Urantia Book*.

"Thou [so-called 'Lucifer'] wast perfect in thy ways from the day that thou wast created…" (Ezekiel 28:15 / brackets added). Consider a few related propositions. Two of the scripture verses that tell of the previously mentioned people, nations, and kingdoms that are eyewitnesses to Lucifer's fall are: "I [God] will bring thee to ashes upon the earth in the sight of all them that behold thee. All they that know thee among the people shall be astonished at thee…" (Ezekiel 28: 18b-19 / brackets added) and "O Lucifer, son of the morning! How art thou cut down to the ground, which didst weaken the nations" (Isaiah 14:12)!

A purpose for using these scriptures that relate to the time when Lucifer fell, thus describing events from the time when the scripturally spoken-of Pre-Adamic humans are eyewitnesses to Lucifer's fall, thus long before Genesis 3, which obviously has no such populations, is that such material also necessarily testifies to an "opposite" of sorts, to the tripartite context of the very *Dispensation of Innocence* that we are presently examining. For if there was a time when Lucifer spiritually fell, and being in view of such contemporary witnesses, as biblically revealed, then there was a pre-fall, an opposite "before time" when Lucifer is perfectly holy amid such other beings. This presence of human-type beings here is not exegetically surprising, but to be expected, as the subsequent two major corresponding template epochs (Adamic and then, subsequently, that of Revelation 21:1) each also have the tripartite makeup corresponding to God's unchanging purposes. It is the ubiquitous world order setup of God.

The act of displacing these so-specified people, nations, and kingdoms to any historical period other than when Lucifer falls (and such efforts are legion) requires violence upon exegesis and thus upon one of its chief pillars—the consideration of the plainly provided perspicuous meaning, thus minus secondary assumptions and like-contrary rhetorical strategizing. Deserving reemphasis, then, attempting to relegate this discussed Pre-Adamic humanoid population of Isaiah 14 and Ezekiel 28 to a time other than the original Pre-Adamic fall, and thereby futilely hopscotching forth with the contention that they are eye-witnessing future Adamites, is similar in its obviousness of error to the life-form identification mistake of micro-anthropomorphically contending that the *elohim* of Psalm 82:1b are also "merely" Adamic humans.

As for Lucifer's "…perfect in your [his] ways from the day you were [he was] created [i.e., created en masse along with all of the other *elohim* spirit-beings at some undisclosed period of time before they witnessed the Genesis 1:1 creation of the heavens and earth / brackets added]," Jack W. Lanford observes, "…All this suggests a wide variety of different manners ('ways') in which he [Lucifer] functioned. And just as important, it suggests time in those services—time unmeasured and certainly not to be convoluted into a few hours or days at the time of his immediate creation. 'Perfection in ways' can only be demonstrated and assessed as a result of an extended period of time during which the many performances can be documented and characterized."

Lucifer's *Dispensation of Innocence* may have lasted for thousands of years. Speculative? Okay. As speculative as gap theory deniers' positing of the creation of angels during the six-day "creation week" (which wouldn't position them for Job 38:7 joy-shout activity), as well as their fall within a matter of days after the creation of Adam, and most unbelievable, that, during that relatively brief time span, Lucifer was able to rack up a "multitude of [not merely sins, but] iniquities"[122] (Ezekiel 28:18a)? So, then, classic gap deniers propose a nonbiblical warp speed creation and fall of Lucifer and company; alternately, what is the evidentiary case for classic gap "theory" proponents?

(1) the exegetic testimony of the sudden and complete Genesis 1:1 creation *contrast to* the step-by-step process for the "six days of creation,"
(2) the free-agent-necessitating telltale devastation of Genesis 1:2, and
(3) an original Eden population of eye-witnesses, all providing exegetic earmarks to the era of the fall of Lucifer.

What imaginings do these deniers of that (above incomplete list) reality have between 1:31 and chapter 3:1 to indicate Lucifer's fall at that time? *Only* unfounded speculation.

Again, the Genesis 1:31's "all things were very good" (but not perfect[123]) retort demands its indoctrinates to close their eyes to the contrary, more sound realizations, such as, "There is no exegetic requirement to justify any insistence that the 1:31 'very good' declaration refers to all previous details of eternal history; rather, it refers only to the 1:3-31 renewal activity, because, for only *one* thing, 1:2's *Targum-Onkelos*-confirmed devastation (that is yet to be discussed in the main text) is certainly not good. Forget the 1:1 epoch for a moment; the point here is, even a highly paid Al Capone defense attorney illusionist-type "gifting" couldn't convincingly turn the meaning of any devastated phenomenon around into any **very** good phenomenon. Thus, a perfectly holy, high society existed quite before the end of Genesis 1:1, to the point of a well-developed culture, including sanctuaries and many other projects of such advancement.

---

[122] *Iniquities* are not merely any degree of wrongfulness, but are commissions of gross wickedness.
[123] "Perfection" is not conveyed in Hebrew by the word *tob* ("good"), but, for example, by the word *tom*.

Figure 2, depicting a lone figure in the forefront, heavily shadowed,
symbolizing the post-perfect, transitional elohim personage who
had begun to question what he had known so well before.

Ezekiel 28:15's operative word, "[un]till" (as in, "Thou wast perfect in thy ways from the day that thou wast created, till…"), is of introductory interest for this dispensation in the sense that it cannot only be used to distinguish the separation from *The Dispensation of Innocence*, its sin-free and perfectly holy quality, but also to distinguish the separation from such sin-free and perfectly holy quality from the onset of the degenerative *phase* that, in itself, precedes the full-blown Devil reputation, that is, from the purer simplicity of the originally perfect form to a more "sophisticated" form that only *began* to lose the element of perfection to increasing degrees, occurring before the first denotative *iniquity* of many more to come.

Contrarily, classic gap-deniers would have Bible students believe that sometime during the ostensibly brief timeframe of Genesis 2, or, as we have discussed, within the single verse of 3:1 itself, *perfect in his ways Lucifer* up and got iniquitously wicked, *multitudinously* so, and apparently, just as spontaneously, pitched the hot-off-the-press muscling-in challenge for other *elohim* to *also* reject God's sovereignty virtually on the spot, to which, a goodly amount of these proposed other *elohim* were like, "Oh, absolutely, we're so yesterday down with that!" Exegetes, or at least those who seriously aspire to that designation, are invited again to continue to biblically evaluate these compared early Genesis perspectives to determine which one is, not the best, but now, which one is *the least ridiculous*. By the way, considering what has been shared, one should already have at least an ever so slight start toward that goal at this time.

Indeed, then, what would come to be known as the fall of Lucifer had an initial phase, a beginning point that came after his "perfect in thy ways" phase, extending up to the time of his first departure from literal perfection. This principle of "departure," of *degeneration*, could be elaborated upon to a great extent, commensurate with the likely significant amount of time that this Luciferian initial phase lasted, but given the principle's no doubt near-universal acknowledgement among intellectually honest types, this work will simply offer a single legitimate axiom and subsequent numerical elaboration that sufficiently and more briefly states the case.

As for the axiom "Sin nibbles at our soul in small steps," blatantly extreme perverseness can spontaneously emerge from perfectly holy beings only after such beings have been deconditioned enough and established into the supplanted inferior nature. Relatably, as inspired by John Witherspoon's sermon on Hebrews 3:13, titled "The Deceitfulness of Sin," an interpretive eight-point summary is offered, suggestive of the timelessly universal principle and process that also, then, relates to the historical and spiritual significance of this second dispensation:

1. One initiates self into a questionable practice, or engages in what may be perceived as lesser infractions.
2. Having once begun in the ways of sin, the person ventures upon something more daring, growing in "courage" with the experience, giving *self* more liberty to walk in the ways of his own less "restricted" heart, rather than in the ways of the Lord.
3. Open sins soon throw the person into the desire for establishing ungodly companions.
4. In this next stage, the sinner begins to experience the force of habit.
5. In this stage, there is a loss of the sense of shame, sinning more openly and boldly.
6. Another stage in the sinner's progress is to harden self so far as to sin without remorse of conscience.
7. If even improved sinners sometimes boast and glory of their former wickedness, it is shameful, and it is one thing to need full deliverance from being stuck in some degree of former shame, but quite another still to so actively glory and revel in ongoing direct wickedness, esteeming it honorable as the ultimate leftist.[124]

---

[124] "The ultimate leftist," in the sense that: "Then shall the King say unto them on his right hand, Come, ye blessed of my Father, inherit the kingdom prepared for you from the foundation of the world...Then shall he say also unto them on the left hand [i.e., biblical leftists], Depart from me, ye cursed, into everlasting fire, prepared for the devil and his angels" (Matthew 25:34 & 41 / bracket added).

8. Not to be content with being wicked alone, the subject uses all their art and influence to make mere sycophant companions into mediators of direct wickedness as well. This is to be zealous in sinning, and industriously, a promoter of interest in the infernal cause.

Dispensation Three: Unrighteous Trade

This dispensation might be connotatively referred-to as "the first multi-level door-to-door pyramid scheme with Satan at the Apex, as CEO." The title for this third dispensation is also in keeping with the Jewish Publication Society of America translation (JPSA), "By your far-flung commerce…" (perhaps edging out the usual KJV phrase, "By the multitude of thy merchandise," of Ezekiel 28:16).

Figure 3, depicting the infamous archangel making another of his pitches to his base

This dispensation's Ezekiel 28:16 theme revolves around the full meaning of the Hebrew word that is translated as "traffick" in the King James, meaning "trading," the term also used in reference to king Tyrus (the Adamic epoch type who was used for alluding to the satanic *elohim* being, inspiring

Ezekiel's prophecy thread), "With thy wisdom and with thine understanding thou hast gotten thee riches, and hast gotten gold and silver into thy treasures: By thy great wisdom and by thy traffick hast thou increased thy riches, and thine heart is lifted up because of thy riches..." (Ezekiel 28:4-5). Again, doctrinally boon companion Jack W. Langford correctly adds, "'By the abundance of your trading you became filled with violence within' (verse 16 / NKJV) ...demands a substantial period of time...a continuum of activity after Lucifer's initial rebellion."[125] Whatever the sum of wealth categories is (that these scriptures allude to), it refers to quite a substantially accumulated amount to say the least. It is comparable to his amassing attribute of false pride itself,[126] a combination underscoring the notable amount of time it took for all of it to add up.

To renew the classic gap theory deniers' challenge to gap theory proponents about including speculation to address related matters of heavenly and earthly timing, consider Perry Stone's teaching about the notorious heavenly kingdom's city of Revelation 21:1, the new Jerusalem. In consideration of Matthew 25:14's "kingdom prepared for you from the foundation of the world," we have an opportunity to first review our established summary of eternal history's beginning timeline elements, including the timing context of the new Jerusalem city's construction. Thus, exegesis establishes the first element of eternal history as God alone before any of his creative activities that are scripturally established, and then subsequently inclusive numbers added here:

1. The various forms of Psalm 82:1b *elohim* are created, as indicated by their eye-witness presence before creation, referred to in Job 38:4-7.

2. "Through faith [rationally justified, so including and transcending the empirical realm] we understand that the worlds were framed by the word of God, so that things which are seen were not made of things which do appear" (Hebrews 11:3 / brackets added). Thus, the heavens and earth are created in Genesis 1:1.

3. Construction of the various components of the kingdom are begun (Matthew 25:14), initiated at the "foundation of the world" beginning part of Lucifer's *Dispensation of Innocence*. (So many millennia later, at the time of Jesus, when he said, in John 14:2, "In my Father's house are many mansions; if it were not so, I would have told you. I go to prepare a place for you," it is apparent that construction or customized enhancements persist, even at the time of Christ.)

---

[125] from, *The Gap is Not a Theory*, page 157

[126] There is no legitimate "true pride," but today, the redundant expression ("false pride") seems necessary because pride is ubiquitously accepted. There is a legitimate point to be made for one to, for example, be transcendently thankful for all manner of great blessings, such as for family members, rather than confess subjectivity to that (pride) which makes one resisted by God (James 4:6).

4. Eventually (in The Pre-Adamic Age), and after the appearance of Pre-Adamic people multiplying to the point of kingdoms and nations on the earth (Ezekiel 28:19 and Isaiah 14:12), likely taking millennia, Lucifer finally yields to the most iniquitous desire, among so many of his previously established multitudes of iniquities, to be as great as God (Ezekiel 28:15).

5. Lucifer corrupts the Pre-Adamic epoch, ultimately resulting in its judgmental destruction in Genesis 1:2.

Perry Stone posits a comparison of the new Jerusalem kingdom city's twelve different levels of "precious stone" material, each type used for a different foundation of that city (listed in Revelation 21:19-20), stones that also incompletely correlate to the nine stones that are part of the high priest "covering" ephod of the Pre-Adamic Lucifer persona (as listed in Ezekiel 28:13). The idea is that the city's Great Architect, God, began overseeing the kingdom's construction project, according to the scriptures, after the foundation of the Genesis 1:1 world is established, and the reason why Lucifer's ephod is not adorned with all twelve of the new Jerusalem's foundation stones could be because Lucifer's ephod is, according to Stone's teaching, progressively enhanced from the very beginning of the kingdom, thus displaying one central stone at first, indicative of the work on the city's first foundation. Then, by the time of that stage in history referred to in Ezekiel 28:13, Lucifer's *Dispensation of Innocence* had lasted only until the ninth level of the city's twelve foundations was complete, thus only the nine stones being infamously memorialized in the ephod tradition, a perpetual reminder of an eternal transition, including the need for a plan of redemption.[127] This perhaps less suspect speculation (than "gap-denier" speculation, even though they also believe in different later gaps) is at least arguably *tied* to a more readily traceable exegetic thread of evidence. Classic gap-deniers have a pittance, if anything, regarding timeframe scriptures or hermeneutical indications thereof to bolster what they imagine about when Lucifer fell.

---

[127] As contractors are said to be the builders because of their production company roles (even though such indicated leaders don't personally perform the bricklaying), so also the "builder and maker [of the new Jerusalem] is God" (Hebrews 11:10 / brackets added) can similarly be understood. And on one level, this is how God's kingdom is "not made with hands" (II Corinthians 5:1), for its essence resides spiritually within its recipients. On the level of the physically manifested kingdom, though, and then in consideration of the Pre-Adamic timeframe of "the foundation of the world" context in which the construction begins to take place (Genesis 1:1), the scriptures do not suggest that the new Jerusalem was instantaneously called into being as the Genesis 1:1 universal cosmos is, availing the significant amount of construction time for the city's first nine levels and beyond. Consider the time it could take to build nine levels of its approximately 1500 miles foursquare dimensions at its base (whether cubical or pyramidal as a whole).

Dispensation Four: Profaned Sanctuaries

The many Ezekiel 28:18 "sanctuaries" of this Luciferian pre-Genesis-1:2 dispensation are physical constructs, as Israel's Adamic-epoch sanctuaries that would also be constructed, for verse 18's original Hebrew term is the same in both of those biblical contexts.

Figure four, depicting the Luciferian degenerative progress, thus
spreading to include even the sanctuaries of that epoch.

The fact that the Pre-Adamic building programs had advanced to the point of including this multiplicity of sanctuaries within the epoch's context of Ezekiel 28:19 nations and Isaiah 14:12 and 16 kingdoms (which would likewise include corresponding complexes of societally supporting architecture of all other kinds), defies the timeline of classic gap deniers. To hold to the belief that all this populace and construction is referring to Adam's Eden, that such items are present near to or within the end of day 6 of Genesis 1 to Genesis 3, requires nothing short of a stiff-necked commitment to a biblically unfounded hermeneutic.

Dispensation Five: Multitude of Iniquities

Ezekiel 28:18 necessitates not only the eventual commission of multitudes of iniquities, but also the formerly alluded-to steps of spiritual degeneration that led up to the very first of many instances of downright iniquity "proper."

Figure 5, depicting the resultant essence from the mounting influence of The (first four) Pre-Genesis-1:2 Dispensations, conveying Lucifer's thematic imagery: "I will ascend into heaven. I will exalt my throne above the stars of God…I will be like the Most High" (Isaiah 14: 13-14).

If classic gap "theory" deniers want to believe that the satan's sum of details that are discussed in these dispensational treatments, that culminate into the "multitudes of iniquities" indictment, manifest as a quick one-shot-deal on day six or a time shortly thereafter, then, in a sense, that shouldn't be surprising for anyone who is familiar with the so many like instances of hermeneutic bizarreness elements that characterize their beginnings-timing model. And, laying aside the point that multitudes of committed iniquities are obviously not indicative of a quick Luciferian fall and of a just as quick, single divine judgment, it then becomes necessary to try to help, by offering the understanding that God's "I change not" nature was not different in the Pre-Adamic epoch compared to its manifestations in the Adamic epoch.

Indeed, then, how does God deal with the most overt forms of Adamic rebellion (that, again, does not zap into a being's makeup in a moment)? Additionally, like The Adamic Age, the Pre-Adamic epoch is also tripartite, consisting, as all three major epochs of eternity consist, of (1) God, (2) lesser *elohim* beings of all types, and (3) human types,[128] so, it is legitimate to recognize the parallels of the epochs in terms of the latter suggested issue of "how does God deal with Adamic epoch rebellion" in order to understand how he deals with free agent rebellion occurring in the initial epoch. If this line of reasoning were not valid, how in the world did Lucifer get past the first iniquity, on to the multitudes of iniquity? He couldn't have. And these multitudes of iniquities had to occur before the time of Genesis 3…long before.

Are there repeated warnings over stretches of time, followed by, "Come, let us reason together" admonitions? All Bible students know that this is the case. Thus, of the five dispensations that occurred throughout The Pre-Genesis-1:2 Dispensations, this fifth one, titled, "Multitudes of Iniquities," may have lasted the longest, perhaps even longer than the first *Dispensation of Innocence*, which presumably could have lasted for millennia. This Multitudes of Iniquities dispensation's theme is akin to God's favored nation of Israel doing "evil in the sight of the Lord," an indictment that is peppered throughout the Old Testament as God worked with them over the course of thousands of years. Given that the Bible is God's plan of redemption for Adamic mankind, the biblical focus is indeed upon the humans in the Old Testament, but, if the purpose was otherwise, as much historical content could surely be available to discuss God's dealing with *elohim* and their human-type counterparts as there presently is for Adamites.

The point is worth reemphasizing: Enough time occurred for *multitudes* of iniquities to be committed during this range of the pre-Genesis-1:2 dispensations, rather than the biblically nonexistent tale of a sudden Luciferian envy about the creation of Adam, temptation, and elohim takeover plan being just as suddenly thwarted within a matter of days. But don't get the applicable bolstering data of the Mesopotamian worldview wrong;[129] it is not being denied that some elohim were indeed put into a snit about the creation and authority of Adam—the point is that the elohim are already fallen long before their latest Adamic epoch screwup. These necessary ranges of time attest to this suggested trans-epochal nature of God that would segment the span of said multitudes of iniquities, punctuating such occurrences within the primordial epoch by using Adamic-dispensation-type warnings and opportunities for repentance. *What*? Repentant fallen *elohim* beings?

---

[128] The post-Revelation-21:1 third epoch's human types are the to-remain non-glorified repentant survivors of the Millennial Reign of Christ who thus enter the new heavens, new earth, and new Jerusalem realm to fulfill the ancient prophecy of eventually, and literally, multiplying the human *natural* (biological human) seed beyond the number of stars that Abraham gazed up to. (It probably wasn't a cloudy night.)

[129] Respectable, though noncanonical, Mesopotamian literature includes detailed coverage of the time when elohim became jealous of Adam's creation, such as I and II Enoch, for example.

This is a reasonable assertion, or so it would seem, especially when considering the conclusion that is due from the existence of *elohim* "elect angels" (I Timothy 5:21) who live in that era—ever since the time even before Genesis 1:1 when they rejoiced about the earth's creation in sync with the appearance of the morning stars. Indeed, it should be understood that some angels became elect in the same way that Adamic humans can become elect, meaning, by having an initially acquired nature of sin, thus existing in a fallen spiritual condition, and then subsequently receiving the plan of redemption that is offered (i.e., the plan of redemption for Adamites being a blood-covenant-based faith, necessitating a repentant reception of Jesus as Savior and Lord, whereas, for example, the plan of redemption for rebel *elohim*/angel beings that were created in the Pre-Adamic epoch is not known, as that particular matter's specifics are not included along with the Bible's other revelations about the Pre-Adamic era[130]).

The collateral information is that some of the fallen *elohim* angels have become "elect" and thus are still favorably active in our Adamic epoch (against the persistently unrepentant number of also yet-active *elohim* beings) and are distinguished from their Pre-Adamic counterpart human types in the sense that no such direct description (as "elect") is provided about their eternal fate.[131] Either the information is not included in the Bible because, unlike angels, Pre-Adamic humans are not nearly as relevant to the Adamic epoch as the yet-present angels are, or because none of the Pre-Adamic human types are redeemed. In consideration of the fact that a saved remnant could have repopulated the epoch with a godlier line of inhabitants who would be wiser about "working with God," along with the fact that the whole epoch was destroyed in Genesis 1:2, and realizing that the Adamic race supplants it, the latter-mentioned fate, indicated in the previous sentence, seems most reasonable. This depth of punishment is not hard to fathom, as the present Adamic order's survival hinged upon the lives of a mere eight souls saved in the ark, the colossal remainder of the planetary population being judgmentally destroyed (also for wickedness).

Adam and Eve encountering a Pre-Adamic ringleader *nachash* satanic form in Genesis 3 seems to signal in every reading of it a need for better answers about that nagging question of why Genesis chapters 1 and 2 themselves provide no fuller explanation about how the pre-Genesis-1:1 Lucifer, the Genesis 1:1 same Lucifer, and the yet one-and-the-same Ezekiel 28:15 "perfect in thy ways" Lucifer could eventually become so corrupt. An important theological principle about

---

[130] However, it is interesting to consider that "the book of life of the Lamb [Jesus] slain from the foundation of the world (Revelation 13:8 / brackets added) occurs, indeed, from "the foundation of the world," the time of The Pre-Adamic Epoch. Is this plan of redemption so-timed because it can apply to such contemporaries?

[131] Granted, hell is created for the devil and his angels, but we know that unrepentant rebels of all types are destined for hell, of course, including Adamites (and so, then, to also include Pre-Adamic human types).

interpreting scripture relates to what message the human author of scripture is intending for readers to understand. The complaint that drawing out an interpretation that the original audience would not have perceived (here, about the origin or circumstances of Lucifer's fall) is a sensible earmark to consider as a buffer against accepting any hastily acquired interpretations, and that valid earmark can be applied to both basic models (i.e., to the classic gap "theory," as well as to its deniers' alternate gap-timing theorizing; neither perception composes an "out of the gate" inherently superior understanding—*that* can be determined only through exegesis).

Apparently, then, for so many, and for so long, it was a non-issue. It was sufficient for the primary purpose of God's redemptive plan for mankind for Genesis 1 to be perspicuously accepted "as is," and to only eventually and inevitably include the knowledge of "the origin or circumstances of Lucifer's fall" timing to become much more broadly available during The Church Age through a maturely developed exegesis based upon the complete canon and corroborating context from ancient worldview content (which contributes to informing biblical authors and compilers), thereby providing what amounts to the incomparable hindsight advantage.

Likely, then, or at least very possibly, the divinely inspired reason or strategy for why Lucifer's story parts are deferred to these much later times in the biblical revelation (besides the reason to prioritize the Adamic story) is to also avail a prevention of sorts, as if to provide a form of insurance. That is, given the Luciferian fall story's timing (its climax occurring at a long time after the very beginning of the 1:1 time, and yet also necessitating the margin of time for Lucifer's spiritual degeneration long before the end of 1:1), followed by the brief declaration of the resultant 1:2 devastation, the narrative's focus is duly abridged to expound upon the earth's six-day renovation for Adam, strictly limiting the details that could otherwise detract from or even confuse for the ancients (and beyond) the main showcase of Adam's and our world.

Put another way, there had to be a buffer, by way of an absence of a highly signaling narrative of details (other than the 1:2 connection to 1:9's tree of the knowledge of evil), to protect against the possibility of complicating said main showcase of Adam, his fall and the promise of redemption. Perhaps the nature of the *Pre*-Adamic plan of redemption that yielded some of those elect angels, if openly laid out in a contextually juxtaposed format with the emergent Adamic plan, could have provided a pattern to be taken more consciously, clueing in the no doubt evilly perceptive forces of darkness about measures that needed to retain their degree of mystery, a la the notorious, "… we speak the wisdom of God in a mystery, even the hidden wisdom, which God ordained before the world unto our glory: Which none of the princes [fallen *elohim*] of this world knew: for had they known it, they would not have crucified the Lord of glory" (I Corinthians 2:7-8 / brackets added). It can be argued that this line of reasoning is speculation, but, again, it emerges from a more consistent hermeneutic than the classic gap deniers' comparatively baseless speculation about their own unadmitted (and thus less honestly embraced) gap theory that they assumptively pitch as being self-evident (regarding their circular reasoning belief about "Lucifer and company's fall occurring between 1:3 and 3:1 because that's when it had to happen").

But much of this theorizing goes beyond the nature of how the authors are inspired when they write scripture. Again, it is not as if the contributing authors of Genesis 1, the most famously recognized compiler being Moses, had or needed the knowledge of The Pre-Adamic Epoch; they simply felt impressed of God's guiding Holy Spirit to record early Genesis as is; this is true irrespective of whether they had knowledge of the former epoch (without the remainder of the biblical canon). So much of scripture is a collection of normal, contemporarily understood, true information. Also, though, at times, and as we have seen, special insight is given to some biblical authors, revealing things that are beyond their ability to know outside of divine revelation from God. For example, all Adam or Moses needed to know about Genesis 1 was that God created the whole natural totality, including the earth (and they may not even have known the planet's general dimensional features), and then that, at some point after the earth's creation, it was devastated and then renovated. For such ancients, anything else is potentially "TMI."

Contrariwise, if Lucifer's fall details were abundantly detailed early in Genesis (instead of completing the story mosaic through holistic canonical exegesis), interpretations about such a theoretical inclusion could still go either way, perhaps to the point of confusing the primary biblical issue of God's plan of redemption exclusively for Adamites; it is as if the door to the full revelation being clearly recognized is made intentionally dependent upon the growth of the Church in establishing well the biblical truths that have finally emerged, meaning, much more widely so, by this point of the last days. This view exalts the scriptures, not eisegesis, and in a way that spares most historical periods from this discussion, apparently one of many discussion-points relegated to the time when "knowledge shall be increased" (Daniel 12:4). This seems like it could be deemed "third party watchdog" more reasonable than its deniers' claims, especially since the extensively sustained debates within Christendom about this topic that are far from the world of the *Targum Onkelos*, let alone far from Adam's and Moses' world, are thus mostly modern occurrences, a modernity that needs to "come into the unity of faith" by way of exegesis. It is hoped that all individuals who have become identified with denying the classic gap theory will not feel that they are presently "too dug in" to turn back now.

12 (from page 26, footnote 44) Given that the far-and-away primary means that God uses to share his will is the Bible, and given that The Pre-Adamic Age is thereby already dependably established,

it is a point of purely add-on interest that a lower or secondary rung means that God is using in these last days to bless his church, also fits the frame of the Genesis 1:1 world being separate and distinct from the Genesis 1:2 (and beyond) world. This refers to the legitimate group of heaven and hell visitation testimonies—of course, only those that are provided by individuals who the God of the Bible uses to warn unbelievers and to encourage believers. Those who deceptively purport to have such visitations are accountable to God.

It is biblically established that the apostle Paul is one of the individuals who is taken to heaven and comes back to earth to talk about it (and other biblical characters are taken bodily to heaven without dying, such as Enoch). Such contemporary visitations today include those who also readily acknowledge that "…all liars shall have their part in the lake of fire…" (Revelation 21:8), so it seems extreme to hold the yet-admittedly-safe position that such personalities would so willingly and blasphemously endeavor to deceive people in the name of Jesus; thus, such testimonies can be taken as special forms of anecdotal reports *when they are in sync with the scriptural record*. Therefore, the next few pages will explore this phenomenon by means of a particular testimony.

For instance, consider a portion of the highly recommended Richard Sigmund testimony, "My Time in Heaven: Full Testimony," wherein he reportedly quotes the words that Jesus spoke to him, commanding him under an assigned prophetic mantle, during his heavenly visitation:

> For centuries men have tried to interpret my word. Some
> were correct in as much light as they had. Some were
> wrong, and some of them were sent by the evil one to lead
> my Father's creation astray. From the day that my grace
> was extended to redeem creation, the evil one has tried to
> steal it from my hands, but until the day that I will soon
> return, that which my Father has committed to me will not
> be taken from me. I have worked to make salvation
> available to all.
>
> I was there when the first rays of my glory created the
> universe—I was there when the planets were made. I did it.
> I created everything to work perfectly after its own order.
> For millennia, everything was perfect; I fellowshipped with
> the first created man in these gardens until sin became a

reality. <u>My Father cast the evil one, and all those who
followed him, into outer darkness.</u> They were cast far
away from this perfect abode that I have prepared for
my bride of faithful believers.

The days of creation are numbered. My Father alone
knows the number of days. He alone. Soon, I will take
the heavenly armies that you have witnessed, along
with the elders that are here, and go to get my people.

Let us begin our discussion with the underlined portion of the narration's second paragraph. From a Young Earth Creationist perspective of the first underlined sentence there, Adam's and Eve's togetherness began six days after the universe was created, and they fellowshipped sinlessly with God for *millennia* thereafter without bearing any children, for it is established that Adam and Eve did not have children until after they were expelled from the garden of Eden due to their sin. However, Cain and Abel were born to Adam before Adam was 130 years old (when Adam had Seth / Genesis 5:3). So we find that Sigmund's report supports the scriptural necessity of the Pre-Adamic race in the sense that the report presents a Pre-Adamic time-frame (i.e., millennia) with "the first created man," interestingly not identified as Adam, details that are sufficient—contrary to the length of Adam's sin-free time-frame—to accommodate the emergence of Ezekiel 28:19 / Isaiah 14:12 people and nations that are eye-witnesses to Lucifer's fall. Thus, the one who God fellowshipped with in perfection for millennia was the first Pre-Adamic man who no longer has any fellowship with God. Thus, notice that in this previous epoch that was sin-free for millennia, Jesus fellowshipped with the first created man (not angel), meaning the first of the Ezekiel 28:19 and Isaiah 14:12 people.

The end-of-Pre-Adamic-fellowship "<u>until</u>" incident of that first underlined sentence certainly also correlates well to Ezekiel 28:15's Luciferian climacteric, "Thou wast perfect in thy ways from the day that thou wast created, [un]till iniquity was found in thee." Further, the same underlined first sentence's detail about the environs (i.e., gardens) in which this unnamed "first created man" inhabited is consistent with the also non-descript degree of Richard's testimony from his first paragraph (i.e., "From the day that my grace was extended to redeem *creation*, the evil one has tried to steal it from my hands"). Again, the statement does not indicate Adam or his race, but the much broader term, God's "creation"; this context includes the angels, and likewise, the Pre-Adamic humanoids.

Adam no doubt continues to fellowship with Jesus, given his legacy of training his children about God's redemptive blood covenant, as evinced in Abel's accepted blood sacrifice (Hebrews 11:4). The non-descript point is also consistent with the second underlined sentence that is kept also interestingly general, not specifying even Adam's *race*. Even though God's offer of a plan of redemption for the original sinners of Lucifer's time may have been different than the biblical blood covenant of Adam's dispensations, the "elect angels" (of I Timothy 5:21 and II Peter 2:4) could very well be, as previously shared, a reference to the same type of chosen ones who, like Adamic elect saints, respond acceptably to whatever God's redemptive offer demanded from those who exist in that initial epoch, indicative of those who had fallen into sin, some of whom (at least some so-specified angels) were then restored into right standing with God.

Another distinction that relates to the above-mentioned "gardens" of the first underlined sentence from the Jesus testimony quotation, is that all *biblical* references to Adam's earthly garden (of Eden) are singular, suggestive of his scaled-down mere section of the restored planet. The postulation here is that the pre-sin original Eden (of Ezekiel 28:13, which is quoted ahead a few paragraphs below) enjoys a higher order of the interdimensional relationship of heaven and earth than what the more probationary limitations of Adam's subsequent Eden allowed, to include not only the whole planetary Eden, but also the Pre-Adamic Eden population's interdimensional capabilities that elohim enjoy, to access the extended gardens of heaven, a precursor form of God's ultimate and original will to enjoin heaven and earth, another epochal mirroring reverberation of a sort, denoting "Thy will...on earth as it is in heaven."

The Richard Sigmund testimony addresses this as well, indeed reverberating Genesis 1:1's astronomically poignant significance of the heaven and earth being singled out from all other elements of the totality:

> Heaven and earth are more connected than most people
> know, and in ways that are beyond our comprehension...
> Heaven and earth are joined at times when the spiritual
> atmosphere and praise and worship are flowing together
> in perfect harmony. When this happens, we are caught
> up into the atmosphere of heaven itself.

This literal crossover phenomenon of earth and heaven is free-flowing in the "pre-until" era of Lucifer's perfect-in-thy-ways holy status. In that earlier part of the Genesis 1:1 realm, God's planetary home headquarters and Earth share a uniqueness above all other cosmic places. Activities in each of these places interact with the other. For instance, revisit this, "Is it heaven or is it earth?" passage from Ezekiel 28:

> [13] Thou hast been in Eden the garden of God; every precious
> stone *was* thy covering, the sardius, topaz, and the diamond,
> the beryl, the onyx, and the jasper, the sapphire, the emerald,
> and the carbuncle, and gold: the workmanship of thy tabrets
> and of thy pipes was prepared in thee in the day that thou
> wast created.

[Compare the latter, ostensibly earthly Eden description, with Revelation 21:18-21's emphasis upon heaven's like-jeweled environs, and then continue with Ezekiel 28's next verse, 14, below.]

> [14] Thou art the anointed cherub that covereth; and I have set
> thee so: thou wast upon the holy mountain of God; thou hast
> walked up and down in the midst of the stones of fire.

[From our above study, we know that "Lucifer" was on the earth; he interfaced with heaven as well, the location of the latter verse 14's "holy mountain of God."]

It is also interesting that Sigmund's final sentence of his second paragraph (on page 140) can be taken two ways. Were "they" cast from "this perfect abode" that was originally prepared for the (Adamic) "bride," or, more exegetically likely, was the abode referring to the Pre-Adamic realm that was *subsequently* reallotted for the redeemed ("bridal") Adamites? The no-doubt intentional vagueness is reminiscent of such other biblical facts of initial intentional vagueness that Genesis reflects about, say, the Genesis 3:15 redemptive promise (so as not to tip off the forces of darkness, which could influence them to refrain from God's great plan to sacrificially crucify "the Lord of glory" / I Corinthians 2:8), and about the matter of precisely when Lucifer's fall occurs.

This largely anecdotal discussion thus also supports the fact of the separate nature of the Genesis 1:1 world compared to the Genesis 1:2 and beyond timeframe. Consider, then, the gap-deniers' thrown-down gauntlet of competing "way out there" stories being sufficiently responded to.

13 (from pages 22 and 30, footnotes 38 and 47) This endnote's material is largely from: https://www.kjvbible.org/satan.html, The Genesis Gap Doctrine of Creationism, or "The 'Gap Theory,'" from Part I – Genesis and Regeneration.

Regarding the Pre-Adamic life forms and related items, consider the introductory truth of the distinguished scientist Maciej Giertych, the Head of the Genetics Department of the Polish Academy of Sciences' Institute of Dendrology. Concerning the origin of races (to function here as a broadly applicable principle distinguishing the Pre-Adamic and Adamic realms) such as the Neandertal race; Giertych writes:

> My primary objection as a geneticist was the claim that the formation of races, of microevolution as it is often referred to, is a small-scale example of macroevolution—the origin of species. Race formation is of course very well documented. All it requires is isolation of a part of a population. After a few generations, due to natural selection and genetic drift, the isolated population will irreversibly lose some genes, and thus as long as the isolation continues, in some features it will be different from the population it arose from. In fact we do this ourselves with artificial selection and creating artificial barriers to generative mixing outside the domesticated conditions. The important thing to remember here is that a race is genetically impoverished relative to the whole population. It has fewer alleles (forms of genes). Some of them are arranged into special, interesting, rare combinations. This is particularly achieved by guided recombination of selected forms in breeding work. But these selected forms are less variable (less polymorphic). Thus what is referred to as macroevolution represents natural or artificial reduction of the gene pool. You will not get evolution that way. Evolution means construction of new genes. It means an increase in the amount of genetic information and not a reduction of it. The evolutionary value of new races or selected forms should be demonstrable by natural selection. However, if allowed to mix with the general breeding population, new races will disappear. The select genes they have will disperse again; the domesticated forms will go wild. Thus there is no evidence for evolution here.

> Currently there are new suggestions that molecular genetics provides evidence for evolution. Analyses of DNA sequences in various species should show similarities between related ones and big differences between systematically far-removed species. They do exactly that. Molecular genetics generally confirms the accuracy of taxonomy. But at the same time it does not confirm postulated evolutionary sequences. There are no progressive changes, say, from fishes to amphibians to reptiles to mammals. Molecular genetics confirms systematics, not phylogeny.

No. Genetics has no proofs for evolution. It has trouble explaining it. The closer one looks at the evidence for evolution, the less one finds of substance. In fact the theory keeps on postulating evidence, and failing to find it, moves on to other postulates (fossil missing links, natural selection of improved forms, positive mutations, molecular phylogenetic sequences, etc.). This is not science. [132]

To expound upon The Pre-Adamic Epoch, consider the truth that, indeed, the old earth and heavens of 1:1 came to an end when they passed into a state of coldness and ruin (about 13,000 - 10,000 radiocarbon years ago). This is at a geological marker point known as the Younger-Dryas cooling event that occurred at the end of the Pleistocene era. Basically, the Earth went cold when the stars in the heavens went dark and cold. In the process, the hydrogen gas of the stars would have been converted to vast quantities of water.[133] That was a source of the waters of the "deep" (i.e., the abyss of the cosmos, besides any subterranean contributions) that overflowed the Earth (in Genesis 1:2). Such an event produces a spectacular light show across the heavens (such as stars expanding into Red Giants and imploding into White Dwarfs, etc.) before the darkness and cold settled in and eventually killed everything on the Earth.

This brings us to the paradox: But when we look up into the heavens today everything appears normal, as if nothing of the sort even happened. Why is that? It is because of a Divine intervention into the workings of the cosmos in sync with the beginning of 1:2. God, who established the observed physical laws of nature, is not himself in subjection to those laws. Our Bible is replete with instances where God intervenes against the normal continuum of the laws of physics and nature. Examples are the parting of the Red Sea (Exodus 14:21), the turning back of the shadow of the sundial (II Kings 20:9), the stopping of the earth's rotation for about 24 hours (Joshua 10:12-14), the virgin birth of the God-Jesus, and his resurrection from the dead. Why should one find it negatively-incredible when God resurrects aspects of the cosmos itself, giving it a renewed "reset" life?

Can such things be explained or defended scientifically? No. Do such things contradict the known observations of physics and chemistry? To the extent we presently know them, yes, they most certainly do. There are some things that cannot be explained by appeals to science;[134] there are many

---

[132] Quoted from SCRIBD's "Pre-Adamic Man," page 9, copyright: Attribution Non-Commercial (BY-NC); originally from: Gerald J. Keane, *Creation Rediscovered*, Credis Pty. Ltd., Doncaster Vic. Australia, 1991, p. 149, in Introduction by Maciej Giertych, pp. 2-4.

[133] For verification, see "Recipe for water: Just add starlight," from the European Space Agency peer-reviewed publication news release, 2-SEP-2010.

[134] Of course, though unacknowledged by indoctrinates of The Darwinian Mythology, the feelings-based philosophical aspects of their Venn-Diagram-clarified religion (of page 110) are also outside the purview of empiricism, though

things that must be accepted on faith because they are beyond the comprehension of mankind's carnal mind. "But Jesus beheld them, and said unto them, With men this is impossible; but with God all things are possible" (Matthew 19:26).

The geologic and fossil records are the surviving evidence that testifies to the truth that the Earth is very old and was populated long before the seven days of Genesis. But does that record provide evidence of the sudden end of the old world by a universal destructive event before the seven days and before Noah's flood? Throughout the geologic record there is evidence of mass extinction and geologic catastrophes. The theory that a giant asteroid struck the earth about 65 million years ago and thus precipitated the demise of the dinosaurs is now widely accepted as a fact. As recently as just a few years ago, that theory was scoffed at until the remains of an ancient crater were found in the Yucatan. That same school scoffed at Alfred Wegner's theory about plate tectonics, "The Origin of the Continents and Oceans," in the early 20th century, but today that theory is considered the grand unifying theory of the geological sciences.

One of the greatest remaining mysteries to modern geology is found within the most recent episode of mass destruction which occurred in the Pleistocene era, the era which is just before the Holocene—the age of Adamic mankind (associated with Genesis 1:2). This extinction event appears to be linked with the Ice Age. The evidence consists of vast "animal cemeteries" found in many places around the world, which seem to show a catastrophic and sudden destruction of life all across the planet, only a matter of a few thousand years ago.

This evidence was documented by many back in the 19th century, but this evidence was mostly ignored by the leading (indoctrinate) scientists of the day because it did not fit into the prevailing "politically correct" paradigm. For the same "reason," this evidence is still mostly ignored today, although the Young Earth Creationists have seized upon it as "proof" of the effects of Noah's flood. It is actually proof of the flood which happened just before the time of Genesis 1:2, the time when all life on the surface of the Earth had been wiped out.[135]

Although there are prudent reasons for one to refrain from subscribing to all the beliefs which the late Arthur Custance put forth in his vast collection of papers (and as applicable to most people's only partially true collections of beliefs), he does present a good argument for the evidence of a great

---

not outside "what passes for" science in today's politically-correct-driven culture that is quite in harmony with and influential/inspirational within such "scientific" industry as we see today.

[135] The best collection of the documentation on this event can be found within the paper "*Catastrophe and Reconstitution*" by the late Arthur Custance.

universal catastrophe in the days before "true man," or Adam, is placed upon the earth. Although the exact mechanics of the total event are not yet understood, there is ample supporting evidence for a vast and violent flood as the destructive agent, meaning a world-event flood before the flood of Noah's day. This would be consistent with the gap of Genesis 1:2 and the condition of the earth at that point in time.

A contemporary perspective, from a published interview and story by Linda Moulton Howe of "Earthfiles," notes that a "12,000-Year-Old Human Hair DNA Has No Match With Modern Humans."[136] Therein, one learns of human hair dating back to the last Ice Age ten to twelve thousand years ago, discovered in 1999 at an archaeological dig in Woodburn, Oregon between Salem and Portland. The Ice Age site is filled with the bones of elephants, sloths, condors and a bird with a 14-foot wingspan. The unidentified human hairs were found perfectly preserved a few feet underground and had enough follicles for DNA analysis. Geology professor emeritus, William Orr, at the University of Oregon, spoke of DNA analysis efforts to match the Ice Age hair to any living hominoid species on earth today, an unsuccessful venture. This reality aligns with the Bible's repeated phrases, "after their kind" and "after his kind" throughout the narrative of Genesis 1's seven days.

Once one grasps the "gap theory" context, and thus when God made the new 1:3 world during those six work days, the Scriptures tell us that God fills the new world with many of the same *kinds* of plants and animals that had been on the face of the Earth prior to Genesis 1:2. Not all kinds were replaced, however, and some new ones that did not exist before were introduced.

The geologic time frame preceding the seven days of Genesis correlates roughly with the end of the great Ice Age at the Pleistocene/Holocene epoch boundary, which dates to about 13,000 - 10,000 radio carbon (*C14*) years before present (i.e., BP).[137] As mentioned previously, the geologic record reveals a mass extinction episode at this time in which hundreds of large and unusual forms of megafauna mysteriously perished from the face of the Earth.[138] Gone were the mammoths, mastodons, giant ground sloths, woolly rhinos, rats the size of dogs, armadillos the size of Volkswagens and about 200 other known species, including dinosaurs. They all disappeared by the end of the Ice Age. Their replacement "kinds" of today (Adam's world) are quite different in both size and morphology.

---

[136] Copyright 2001 by Linda Moulton Howe - All Rights Reserved. From: bfro.net/gdb/show_article.asp?id=261 / media Article # 261, Tuesday, August 28, 2001

[137] This "BP" refers to 1950 AD, when the standard astronomical epoch usage was inaugurated.

[138] See: Ice Age Mammals Printouts - EnchantedLearning.com

Scientists have postulated many "possible" explanations for the reason why there are such differences in "kind." A leading theory was that humans hunted these large animals to extinction. Some hold to the belief that they were killed off by disease or their inability to adapt to a changing post-glacial climate. Consider the visual aids below.

Paleoclimate and GISP2 Volcanic Markers

Data From GISP2 Greenland Ice Sheet Volcanic Markers

There are two important things one may note from the composite graphic above. The top chart shows global temperatures across time while the bottom chart shows Sulfate levels in the atmosphere across the same period of time. The latter, the SO4 ion level, is a paleo-proxy volcanic activity indicator. Points to observe:

I.   There is an increase in volcanic activity between when the megafauna extinctions begin (about 14,000 BP), and when they end, a little over 7,000 years ago. That would be roughly one-thousand years before the Earth is pronounced "without form, and void," the end of *that* time being about 6,000 years ago (i.e., the time of Genesis 1:2's end).

II. The megafauna extinction phase terminates in a relatively sudden and dramatic drop in global temperatures, marked by the mentioned Younger-Dryas cooling event.

Clearly, the data indicate there were rapid temperature changes, an onset of intensive geologic activity, and probably changes in the levels of solar activity at this point in Earth's history. The latter probability is supported by reported fluctuations in radiocarbon concentrations in the Younger-Dryas cold period between 12,700 and 11,500 years BP. In addition, abundant tiny particles of diamond dust have been found in sediments dating to 12,900 years ago at six North American sites. This latter observation adds strong evidence for Earth possibly being impacted by carbon-and-water-rich comets or carbonaceous chondrites (asteroids or meteors) at the time of the Younger-Dryas.[139]

Unfortunately, the biblical report of the universal catastrophic destruction of all living things in the recent geologic past (of about 12,000 years ago), followed by a supernatural regeneration of the face of the Earth, along with the restoration of its surface flora and fauna by God, is not something that the many *politically correct* men and women of "science" would even consider to be within the context of the Scientific Method (irrespective of the truth that their own left side of the Venn Diagram is less empirically justified than that of Intelligent Design advocates). So, one may expect, as ubiquitously precedented, even more new theories to emerge as such scientists continue to opine about this problem of theirs. And it does present problems, in reasoning and common sense:

Would it not seem logical that a catastrophic event of this magnitude and severity, which wiped out the giant mammals, would also wipe out the humanoids that hunted them? That would call into question the validity of the scientific theories that those so-called nomadic hunters, who are supposed to have killed off the megafauna, subsequently emerge from the Ice Ages, giving up hunting and taking up agriculture. If they died off too, though, then Adam and Eve were simply not descended from those humanoids. There could be no so-called evolutionary link.

Obviously, if the Paleoclimate data are valid, and the biblical timeline of Adam and modern mankind is valid, then we must conclude that those perished beings were on the face of the Earth before Adam and Eve. But who and what are they? Well, we do know biblically that the angels were the Earth's early inhabitants, along with the humanoid subjects of the main text's discussion about the Ezekiel 28 and Isaiah 14 nations and people. Whether or not some of these archaeologically implicated "subjects" were the fleshly descendants of some fallen angels that existed later in that Pre-Adamic Epoch, thus biological hybrids as occur in the Genesis 6 context, we cannot know for sure at this time. But what we can know is those beings were not any descendants of Adam and Eve,

---

[139] For reports concerning this possibility of cosmic impacts causing Younger Dryas extinctions, see: https://www.sciencedaily.com/releases/2019/03/190313140616.htm

as Young-Earth Creationists are forced to claim (a la their unbiblical 6000-year proposal for the age of the universe, thus not able to recognize the existence of the previous humanoid civilization).

DNA testing of Neanderthal remains clearly shows that modern man is not descended from the Neanderthal; the DNA from three different sets of Neanderthal remains show that there is no genetic link between modern man and the Neanderthal; more recent studies of Neanderthal and Neanderthal skull characteristics further confirm this finding.[140]

The remains of an "anatomically modern human" (Cro-Magnon), found in Australia, have revealed that it was at least 60,000 years old and had a *mitochondria* DNA generic marker which is now extinct; that is, nobody today is descended from that particular line of beings, at least on the *female* side. This find has raised serious debate between the "Out of Africa" and "Regional Continuity" evolutionary camps.

Although there have been relatively recent reports of finding Neanderthal DNA segments in the DNA of some of the Earth's modern human population, this does not conclusively prove that Neanderthals and modern man mated sometime in the past. There is, again to allude to the Genesis 6 occurrence (and as intimated in Daniel 2:43 et al.), another plausible, precedented explanation concerning the exploits of the fallen angels. Angels always appear as men throughout the Bible. And in order to create any offspring with human women, they too must have suitably unique DNA compatible capability. If Genesis 6:2-4 is indicative of such behavior in Noah's day, and thus as Daniel 2:43 hints of such behavior in more recent times (or rather, in the near AD 21st century future, as Daniel's prophecy targets), then it is a possibility that those same elohim "sons of God" could have been up to those same tricks with the bipedal biologics that inhabited the Pre-Adamite world.

Reasoning from the politically correct uniformitarian paradigm (i.e., The Darwinian Mythology), and in reference to the above-cited pro and con cases of DNA connections to present humans, such secular scientists say that this only means that those particular lines of humans must have been a branch of mankind that perished. They would have to make the claim that, as evolutionary notion demands, there was continuity of the human race. However, the link between the evidence from the past and present is still yet to be "scientifically" established—or rather, meaning, *non*-scientifically established, as referring to the irrational religion of atheism, but—yet to be *empirically* established. In fact, evolutionary research is finding just the opposite of their preferences, when not considering their secondary fix-it assumptions. Today scientists are claiming that human evolution has greatly

---

[140] See: Neandertal DNA - Archaeology Magazine Archive and BBC NEWS | Science/Nature | Blow to Neanderthal breeding theory and BBC NEWS | Science/Nature | Neanderthals 'not close family'.

accelerated, particularly since about 10,000 years ago.[141] The truth is, there are big morphological differences between "modern man" (i.e., Adamic) and "primitive man" (i.e., Pre-Adamic), and pronouncing a sudden acceleration of evolution is their only way of desperately explaining the findings within the embraced sacred cow of the evolutionary paradigm.

The Bible has a better answer: Modern man is a new creation, a new creation made in God's image and placed on the face of the regenerated Earth. The concisely parsed words of the Holy Bible say that there is a gap, or discontinuity, between the ancient world of the past (which includes the so-called Neanderthal and Cro-Magnon) and the present world of modern Adamic mankind. The very existence of such a gap in the Genesis narrative is the unifying factor between the Bible narrative and the observations of geology and paleontology. With its steadfast rejection of knowledge that a "gap" exists, mainline science must religiously assume that there is a continuum of life and is forced in the futile attempt to fill in the blanks with whatever available evidence and theories they can find in order to explain their demonstrably incoherent worldview.

Leaving behind the obscure and mysterious events of the Pleistocene epoch and the geologic ages that came before it, let us now examine God's handiwork of the six days of the Genesis restoration of life. On the third day God replenished the earth with vegetation:

> And God said, Let the earth bring forth grass, the herb yielding
> seed, [and] the fruit tree yielding fruit after his kind, whose seed
> [is] in itself, upon the earth: and it was so (Genesis 1:11 /
> brackets added).

> And the earth brought forth grass, [and] herb yielding seed after
> his kind, and the tree yielding fruit, whose seed [was] in itself,
> after his kind: and God saw that [it was] good (Genesis 1:12 /
> brackets added).

Notice the phrase, "after his kind"—which does, after all, necessitate "after"—indicative of what God is presently putting on the Earth during the six days being modeled after the same kind of plants that were on the earth before. They were made after the kinds of things that were here before.

On the fourth day God makes the sun, moon and stars fully operational again, from the ruins of

---

[141] See: BBC NEWS | Science/Nature | Human evolution is 'speeding up'

the old cosmic order. The fact that the Bible says God made the vegetation on the third day and the sun on the fourth day causes some Bible critics to point out that plants need sunshine to grow (photosynthesis), so "the sequence can't possibly be true." Given that the seven days of Genesis are literal 24-hour days, though, of course, there is no problem here. Since there were less than 24 hours between the placement of the vegetation (on day 3) and the making of the regenerated sun (on day 4), as any farmer can testify, all plants can survive 24 hours without any sunlight; they've been doing so for half of a day every day for quite a while now, with no insurmountable problem. Of course, this order of events (the plants before sunshine) also legitimately disallows the notion that the seven "days" are long periods of time or that the Genesis account roughly parallels the geologic record. It does neither. Please, one must restrain the leaps of secondary assumptions to be forced into one's preconceived preferences.

On the fifth day God fills the oceans with fish and aquatic mammals and fills the skies with birds:

> And God said, Let the waters bring forth abundantly the moving
> creature that hath life, and fowl that may fly above the earth in the
> open firmament of heaven. And God created great whales, and
> every living creature that moveth, which the waters brought forth
> abundantly, after their kind, and every winged fowl after his kind:
> and God saw that [it was] good (Genesis 1:20-21 / brackets added).

Again, the "after their kind" is presented, this time concerning the creatures in the sea, and the birds. The Bible shows that modern birds are not the direct descendants of the dinosaurs, a baselessly ludicrous proposition.[142]

According to the fossil record interpretations, there have been life forms in the earth's oceans for millions of years. Many are long since extinct and new kinds took their place over the geologic ages. There are also fish that scientists thought were long extinct, but which have been found alive in today's oceans. The Coelacanth is the best known example. A few years ago, there was great excitement over the claim that scientists had discovered a living prehistoric Coelacanth. However, later, when scientists compared the fins of a fossilized Coelacanth with those of ones caught off the coasts of Africa and Indonesia, it turned out that it was not really the same primitive fish.[143] It would appear that this "chap" too was made "after his kind," and thus was not a direct descendant of the fossilized examples. In God's creative restocking of the new world's oceans on that day, God

---

[142] See: Did feathered dinosaurs exist? | EurekAlert!
[143] See: Fossil Fin Sheds Light on Evolution of Limbs | Live Science

sees fit to include a fish akin to the old Coelacanth *kind* along with other *kinds* of fish which have populated the Earth's seas in the times immediately prior to the old world's destruction. On the other hand, many other ancient marine species were not reintroduced in the regeneration.

Then there is the sea creature that God created that was *not* made "after his kind," but was introduced as a unique creation in the new world, the "great whale":

> And God created great whales, and every living creature that
> moveth, which the waters brought forth abundantly, after their
> kind, and every winged fowl after his kind: and God saw that it
> was good (Genesis 1:21).

Notice in the sentence structure of Genesis 1:21 that the creation of the "great whales" is set apart from the making of the rest of the sea creatures. Are the great whales a specific species of the whale like the gigantic *Blue Whale*, or is this a general reference to the suborder of *Baleena* or to a particular size range? That is not provided in the scriptures. There are small whales that look like dolphins, like the *Beluga Whale*. And there is a larger animal we call a killer whale, or Orca, which is actually the largest dolphin. And then there is the Whale Shark, which is not a mammal like the whale or dolphin (it is a really big fish). So the biblical expression "great whales" is somewhat ambiguous. Regardless, we can say with a high degree of confidence that, according to the Bible, there are "great whales" swimming in today's oceans that were not a part of the earth in the Pre-Adamic Epoch.

On the sixth day, the Lord filled the new world with the land animals:

> And God said, Let the earth bring forth the living creature after
> his kind, cattle, and creeping thing, and beast of the earth after
> his kind: and it was so. And God made the beast of the earth
> after his kind, and cattle after their kind, and every thing that
> creepeth upon the earth after his kind: and God saw that [it was]
> good (Genesis 1:24-25 / brackets added).

Again, all these living creatures (like the vegetation) are said to be made "after their kind" or "after his kind," and, by means of such consistent repetition, there is a great telltale emphasis placed on that point in the narrative. Now, and this is crucial; let us see what else God did *not* make "after his kind," which is man:

And God said, Let us make man in our image, after our likeness: and let them have dominion over the fish of the sea, and over the fowl of the air, and over the cattle, and over all the earth, and over every creeping thing that creepeth upon the earth (Genesis 1:26).

It should be pointed out that *man* is the only living thing in Genesis (other than the whale) that is not said to be made "after his kind"; therefore, he is new and unique, certainly not patterned after the Pre-Adamic humanoid to any noteworthy degree, although bipedal, etc. (and sharing other superficial, mere general physical parallels: two eyes, having a seminal "seed within" quality, whatever[144]). That uniqueness is, then, in respect to being made in the image of God. This manner of improved man is to replace the humanoids that inhabit the old world.

So, "true Modern Man" is a newcomer to the face of this old planet. True Man, made in the image of God, has only been on the Earth about 6,000 years. He is created, not evolved. Although he is preceded on the face of the earth by lineages of humanoids of varying morphology closely approaching modern anatomical similarity, Adam and his descendants (us) are unique.

14 (from page 36, footnote 54) Mt. Saint Helens strata

Mount Saint Helens released the energy of 20 million tons of TNT on the morning of May 18, 1980. The blast pulverized rock and ejected tons of steam-infused ash and sediments throughout that day. Over three billion cubic yards of avalanche material slid down. Eventually, the muddy wreckage settled. At this point, the expectation could be that the debris would settle haphazardly. However, a 1982 mudflow carved deep channels through the thick Mt Saint Helens 1980 deposits, exposing mud made solid in just two years. It was irrevocably confirmed that the initial explosion formed distinct layers. Giant cross-beds and fine, flat layers both formed fast. It thus becomes evident that it does not take millions of years to make such layers, such strata. You just need plenty of fast-moving water.

The Mt. Saint Helens-associated events only needed months to form the same features found in sedimentary rocks around the world. Common features include:

- sharp, flat contacts between layers;
- larger particles toward the bottom of a rock bed;

---

[144] The real idea here is that Adamic humans have within a unique "breath of life" from God quality that Pre-Adamic forms do not have.

- cross-beds;
- steep-walled canyons;
- drainage systems;
- material moved far away before becoming part of new rock;
- de-limbed, sorted, and reburied logs (that heretofore, being buried at different mounting levels of the same deluge sedimentary material, have been mistaken for different forests existing during differing geological eras); and
- volcanic ash mixed with mud and hardened into rock.

Noah's flood, not to mention the Pre-Adamic flood, could have produced enormous strata stacks within one year. We don't need long ages to solidify sediments. But what about the age-dating schemes that supposedly prove those ages?

Within six years of the eruption, a new lava dome in the crater atop Mt. Saint Helens had hardened. Standard radioisotope methods pointed to an isotopic age of around 350,000 years for the 10-year-old rock.[145] The highly regarded radioisotope dating methods are broken.[146] This made the relatively recent 1:2 flood, as well as Noah's flood that much more sensible.

If rock layers form fast, then the earth's age wasn't necessarily as old as The Darwinian Mythology and like models claim—*meaning*, as someone once said, not enough time for "goo to zoo to you." (However, though the earth's age is in doubt in consideration of Darwinian assumptivism, the earth is indeed far older than the 6,000 years that Young Earth Creationists erroneously postulate.) The further along legitimate science advances in debunking the mechanism of the mythology's mathematically impossible timeframe (as legitimately accomplished in endnote 2) the further one comes along in debunking the associated proselytes' non-empirical religion.

It cannot be overemphasized to view/invest-in the video below, which goes in-depth into the empirical science of the Mt. Saint Helens incident, "God's gift to creationists"; if you watch this, you will be taken aback, and downright empirically gleeful that you didn't overlook it:

***https://answersingenesis.org/store/product/mount-st-helens/

---

[145] Morris, J. and S. A. Austin, 2003. *Footprints in the Ash*. Green River, AR: Master Books, 25.
[146] See Dr. Vernon Cupp's book, *Rethinking Radiometric Dating: Evidence for a Young Earth from a Nuclear Physicist.*

15 (from page 36, footnote 55) Regarding the two true perspectives related to the extreme acceleration of time phenomenon, consider the following modified response from "Sir titus 213."[147]

In March 2016, it was announced that the Hubble space telescope spotted the oldest galaxy ever found. Scientists say we're seeing its light as it was sent 13.4 billion years ago. They also believe this was about 400 million years after the Big Bang. This means that scientists believe our universe is about 13.8 billion years old (400 million = .4 billion).[148]

Scientists also know, thanks to Hubble, that the universe is expanding from its origin, like a balloon being blown up. The result of the stretching of space produces the effect that when observing a series of events that took place deep in space, far from our own galaxy, as the light from those events travels through space, the timing of the sequence of events is also actually stretched out. It's like what happens to two dots drawn 1-inch apart on a deflated balloon; as the balloon is inflated, the two dots are no longer only 1 inch apart.

Astronomers have determined that space has stretched by a factor of 900 billion since its origin. Here's what this means. Imagine that you sent out a pulse of light the day after what science calls "the Big Bang," and then another pulse 1 second later. Now suppose that here on earth one of our huge dish telescopes just picked up your first pulse. Would the next one come 1 second later? No, it would come 900 billion seconds later because of the stretching of space.

Some Bible-believing scientists have suggested that when Genesis talks about the six days of re-creation "reset" (or "renovation," which were six literal 24-hour days at the time) it looks forward in time from the Creator's perspective, from time-space coordinates right after the cosmic reset. Since then, the universe has expanded out. Space stretches, and that stretching of space totally changes our perception of time. As we look <u>backward</u> in time, we have to adjust for this stretching-out effect. According to Genesis 1, Adam was created after the 5th day, but before the end of the 6th day of creation.

5.5 days of renovation reset x 900 billion (the expansion factor) = 4,950,000,000,000 days. Since we're talking regular 24-hour days, we divide 4,950,000,000,000 by 365 days in a year, which comes out to 13.6 billion years. Considering that Genesis 1:3-31 works with only six periods of (day) time, the numerical agreement being in such proximity to the suggested figures is interesting. The

---

[147] See: titus 213, posted Thu Apr 27, 2017, on "http://www.kjvbible.org/satan.html."
[148] http://www.usatoday.com/story/tech/nati ... /81309004/

universe is billions of years old, but those billions of renovation "reset" years compress down to the five and a half, 24-hour days.

16 (from page 43, footnote 61) early evidence for the so-called gap theory

The graphic below is from the mid-14th century AD *Sarajevo Haggadah*, depicting the historical timeframe extending from the chaos (of 1:2) through Day 7 of Genesis 1:31.[149] This, then, illustrates the biblical fact of a chaotic earth existing before the 6 Days "of creation," further necessitating one's recognition of the Adamic timeframe beginning with 1:3's Day 1 when God brings nothing new upon the previously established scene except light, for the earth and its preexistent darkness is already there. This term, "preexistent," is meant to convey the biblical truth that the verses before 1:3 are not to be included with the chronology of Adam's genealogical line that is described in Scripture, reflecting approximately 6000 years from Adam to the present 21st century AD. The premier principle of the *previous* 1:1 (through 1:2) timeframe can be better understood in the meaning of its operative word, "beginning," akin to such Scripture usages as, for example, in "I am the Alpha and the Omega, the beginning and the end" (Revelation 1:8), denoting the unmeasured past.

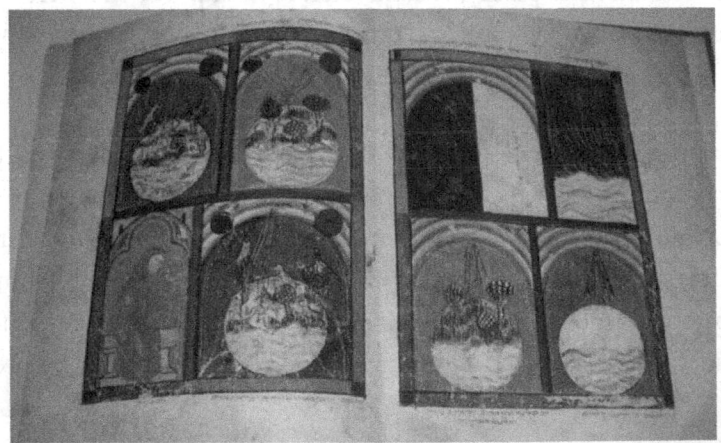

---

[149] Of course, consistent with the Hebrew method of reading from right to left, the upper right frame depicts the 1:2 chaos, and the next frames, starting there to its immediate left, are Days 1-3; and then for the lower row starting at the far right again, the Day 4 through Day 7 is seen.

The diagram below is another example of early evidence for the Pre-Adamic Epoch.

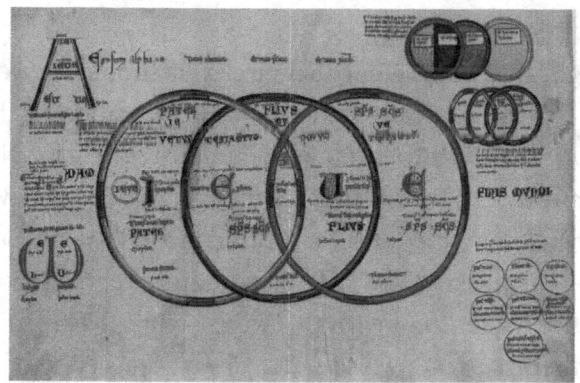

Depicted above is the Liber Figurarum, or TAVOLA XI, featuring the central
Trinitarian circles; uppermost right, a design indistinguishable from the established
"original creation, primeval fall; Adamic renovation; and re-creation."

Thirteenth century Joachim of Fiore produced a body of material including the above TAVOLA XI, reflecting his priority to deal with what this work labels as "Epoch II" matters, meaning with things since the time when Adam is created, extending to the end of the world-under-human-government (i.e., from Genesis 1:3 through Revelation 20:6[150]), thus, not overtly addressing Epoch I or III. Like Genesis 1's speedy summary over former (1:1-2) things before moving right on to the Adamic epoch, then, Joachim relegates a mere headnote in the uppermost right in the above image—the three overlapping circles—graphically centralizing the Adamic epoch, the middle circle (or Epoch II period), the shadowy dark green Adamic world. Notice the more lifelike green of the far left half of the far left circle, and the deathly dark of the right half of that far left circle. The "more lifelike green" intermittent part there of that far left circle half, imperfectly reflects the bright green wholeness of the far right circle, Epoch III. These two end-caps are indicative, respectively, of the far left circle's Genesis 1:1's perfect and complete beginning, which then "somehow" becomes Genesis 1:2 devastated…(followed by The Adamic Epoch in the midst)…followed by God's finally fulfilled original vision for the perfect world of Revelation 21:1 to exist forever.

Florina Rodica Hariga notes, "It is difficult to render a conclusive analysis of…Joachim's treatise… [as it] is now lost. The work may only be observed by analyzing fragments… Regardless of what might have been written in the lost work, the clearest image of the Trinity and of the interpretation

---

[150] Human government will end at the Millennial Reign; however, all negative traces of former-natured human government will be forever gone at the time of the new heaven, new earth, and new Jerusalem (i.e., Revelation 21:1 and beyond).

of the doctrine expressed by Joachim remains the one present in Liber Figurarum depicting the Trinitarian circles."[151]

As for the uppermost right overlapping epochal circles, it should be well-understood that part of Joachim's Trinitarian focus includes his universal incorporation of the John 16:13 principle, the availability of the Spirit of truth to guide one into all the truth, spiritually, physically, and historically. Gabor L. Ambrus expounds, "In like manner, Joachim views (the doctrine of) the Trinity as a guiding principle or a medium (or a fundamental diagram), in which and through which the whole truth will be given to us."[152] Thus, Joachim's reputation as the analogical seer of "all things trinary," is entirely consistent with this work's biblical Three Epochs, and then each of these three epochs with their tripartite world order, always consisting of God, lesser elohim, and humanoids.

The latter two examples of early evidence acknowledging the early Genesis gap may be considered as an introduction to the most ancient textual evidence of a time gap; that being Genesis 1:1-2, exegetically speaking.

17 (from page 44, footnote 62) In consideration of toledoth and colophon data, Adam was the original author of Genesis 1.

The book of Genesis is divided into sections by the "These are the generations of..." phrase (or synonymous expressions). These "generations," or *toledoth* [in Hebrew] type usages, consistent with the end-phrase colophons in other pre-Abrahamic ancient tablets, name the writer or owner of the tablet at the end.[153] In other words, Genesis sections originally exist as sets of tablets, each written by the eyewitness contemporary to the events described, and finally compiled by Moses and others. For example, Genesis 2:4's, "These are the generations of the heavens and of the earth when they were created, in the day that the Lord God made the earth and the heavens," when understood in conjunction with the very next *toledoth*, Genesis 5:1's, "This is the book of the generations of Adam...," makes it apparent that God (from 2:4) directly provided Adam with the revelations that he couldn't have known independently. These revelations thus enable Adam to author the information from the earliest chapters

---

[151] From pp. 292-293 of META: RESEARCH IN HERMENEUTICS, PHENOMENOLOGY, AND PRACTICAL PHILOSOPHY VOL. XI, NO.1 / JUNE 2019: 287-295, ISSN 2067-3655, www.metajournal.org Joachim of Fiore's Symbolical Depictions of the Trinity and the Interpretation according to the Principle of Similitude * Florina Rodica Hariga "Babeş-Bolyai" University of Cluj-Napoca.

[152] from page 620, of "Diagrammatic Design and the Doctrine of the Trinity," in Joachim of Fiore.

[153] "Colophon" is the ancient tablet synonym of Hebrew "*toledoth*" usage.

of Genesis, thus bolstering the case that such recording is from first-hand knowledge and experience. All such records were passed on, and, to name one key personality, collected by Noah, to continue to preserve for posterity, eventually being compiled into the form that we know today as the Bible.

Judging by the so-preserved biblical chronologies, Adam's grandson Enosh, for example, is a contemporary of Noah for eighty-four years, and so could have providentially known him personally. Likewise, Lamech, contemporary of Adam for fifty-six years, and son of Methuselah, is Noah's father. Noah's sons are alive when Abram is born. Using such processes of noting the number of years a person lives and their age when they father the son recorded in the biblical genealogies, we are also able to determine many other notable historical insights, including, for another example, that from Adam's creation to Noah's death, 350 years after the flood, is about 2000 years (circa 2000 BC).

18 (from page 71, footnote 83) The tabernacle system is formalized with the establishment of Levitical law during the wilderness wandering after the Exodus from Egypt. The system's initiating seed of inspiration is the Genesis 3:15 promise of a prophetic Coming of the Messiah who fulfills the ultimate form of innocent blood sacrifice. Thus, the tabernacle system is "a shadow and type" that looks ahead to repentant biblical faith in the blood of Jesus, established as the only means by which anyone can be saved; that's the only way any person can become "in Christ" (II Corinthians 5:17). Indeed, "If you don't have the son [Jesus], you don't have the father [God]" (I John 2:23 / brackets added). Given that salvation has been arranged and offered, the human place in God's scheme should be clarified. Following, is a biblical overview of the human situation (as also composed by this book's author):

> God created a perfect world that became very sinful and
> spiritually dead due to rebellion against God's word; thus,
> all humans are born with an inherited nature of sin,
> completely incompatible with God. Motivated by his own
> great love, though, God put the first and only legitimate
> "religious" plan into action whereby the spiritually fallen
> ones could be forgiven and thereby become spiritually
> reborn, thus "saved," restored into right-standing with God
> as it was before the original fall into sin.

Religious branch-offs (or entirely unrelated disconnects) from the original biblical plan for eternal salvation that ultimately embodies the Old and New Testaments are soul-destroying "departures

159

from the faith" (I Timothy 4:1). In the Old Testament, a saved status occurred for individuals who accepted God's truth by faith, his truth that has been prophetically fulfilled according to the scriptures. Of course, the Old Testament plan began with Genesis 3:15's innocent animal sacrifices that functioned as substitutes for the guilty people (Adam and Eve) who sought forgiveness. For a good biblical summary of this Old Testament progression to New Testament blood sacrifice topic, read Hebrews 9:22-28. The guilty people who offer the animal sacrifices are not examined or judged for imperfections, the animal sacrifices themselves are judged, and thus, to be used, the animals that are substituted for human guilt have to be free of (physical) imperfections. (See the book of Leviticus for priestly details that relate to this ceremonial practice.) Animal sacrifices did provide a temporary forgiveness of sins, restoring the faithful who lived in that time to a right relationship with God.

With the coming of Jesus, the New Testament fulfilled the long-prophesied promise of a better covenant. Now, with the innocent blood sacrifice of Jesus, believers have—not mere temporary forgiveness as the animal sacrifices provided, but eternal forgiveness on Judgment Day because, this time (with the New Covenant instead of the Old), the impeccable righteousness of Jesus is substituted, judged in place of the believers' unrighteousness, and, also mind-blowing, believers thus enjoy a joint-heir status (inheriting the limitless resources of the totality) forever with the King of kings, Jesus himself!

Non-acceptance of God's lone plan for forgiveness through Jesus Christ equates to such an individual's insistence on personally paying the price for sin (consciously suffering in hell forever), a foolish choice given that the price for sin has already been paid in full, necessitating the individual's repentant acceptance during "life's probationary period," referring to the individual's natural lifespan, after which, the individual is judged by God based not upon behavior, but first, upon whether the individual received God's offered single means of forgiveness through Jesus. So, individuals would be much better off in the long (eternal) run if they did it Yahweh, not their own way.

Sin is an eternal offense, to say the least, an ancestrally inherited pathological condition that is infinitely contrary to God's nature, so the punishment of hell certainly fits the crime. The less that one understands this, the more it underscores the great degree to which humans inevitably fail to comprehend just how unsurpassably horrible and consequential sin really is; so the typically cavalier attitude that people convey about this topic is a great irony. Sin is infinitely poisonous, nothing able to immunize against it except its only true opposite—the blood of God-Jesus himself. That is why it is inaccurate to conclude that foolish rebels going to hell for eternity is the ultimate example of overkill. Because we are incapable of understanding the nature of the evil that is passed down from Adam to all humans, we thereby have a carnal incapacity that works against the truth that it is proper and right for God to eternally condemn to hell those who choose to remain outside of Christ.

19 (from page 116, at the end of endnote 2) For a variety of more truly-as-empirically-conclusive material, see Stephen C. Meyer's books:

(1) Return of the God Hypothesis,
(2) Signature in the Cell, and
(3) Darwin's Doubt.

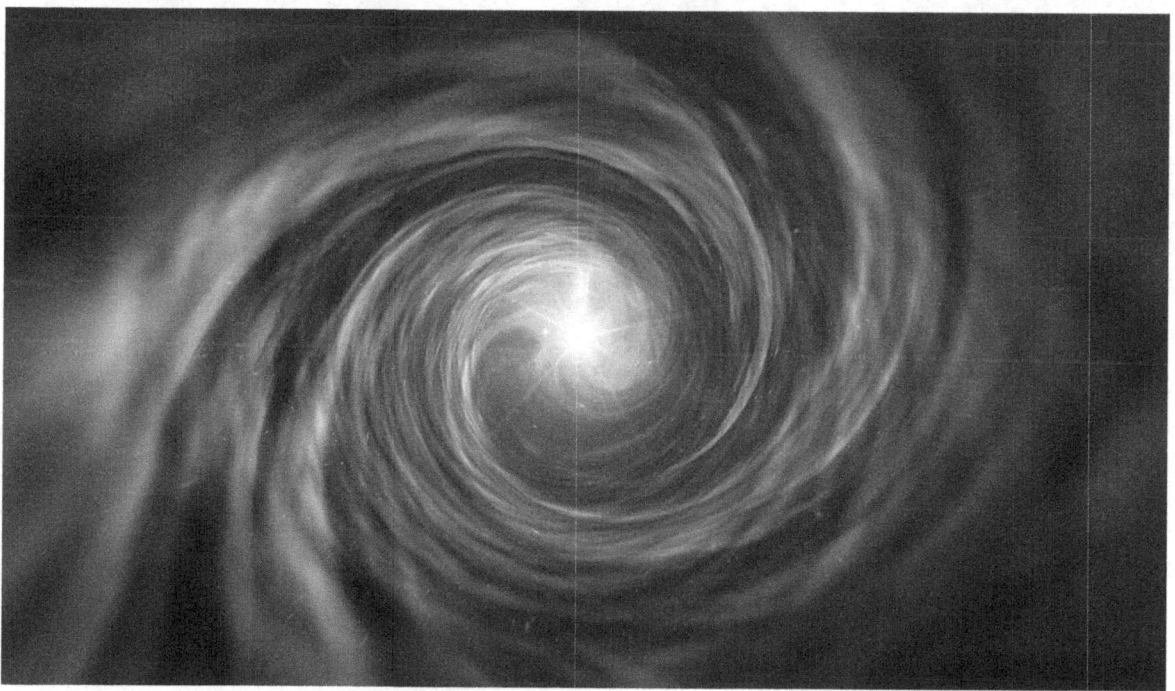